PRAISE FOR *SCARED BY THE BIBLE*

"Through sophisticated, mirthful writing, Prof. Grafius brings his vast knowledge of horror to his deep critical engagement with the Bible. The result is a brilliant examination of the ways in which horror narratives help us to imagine new possibilities."

—*Robin R. Means Coleman, professor of media studies and African American and African studies, University of Virginia, author of* The Black Guy Dies First: Black Horror Cinema from Fodder to Oscar

"Once again, Brandon Grafius has shown us that we are not done with religion and horror, that the inextricable relationship between them has much to teach us about ourselves as believers. . . and as those who look askance at faith-based optimism. *Scared by the Bible* should be essential reading for anyone interested in why we believe what we believe, why we continue to fear the things we do, and the inescapable links between them."

—*Douglas E. Cowan, professor of religious studies and social development studies, Waterloo University and author of* America's Dark Theologian: The Religious Imagination of Stephen King

I0806639

"You don't need to be a theological scholar to find this book fascinating—not if you're curious about the horrors of our existence, and how storytellers have grappled with those horrors for millennia. An absolutely engaging and thought-provoking read."

—*Zoje Stage, USA Today bestselling author of* Baby Teeth *and* Wonderland

"A thoughtful exploration of fear, faith, and storytelling. If, like me, you're a horror fan who grew up asking difficult questions in Sunday school, this book has your name on it."

—*Matt Ruff, author of* Lovecraft Country

"*Scared by the Bible* deftly connects Jason Vorhees to the Book of Numbers, posits Godzilla as a modern day Leviathan, and welcomes readers into the Last House of the Lord on the Left, just to name a few miracles found within its pages. Brandon Grafius shows us that the blood red line that divides a house of worship from the grindhouse is razor thin, and I'm here for every slash of it."

—*Clay McLeod, Chapman, author of* Wake Up and Open Your Eyes

"With imagination, clarity, and verve, Brandon Grafius's *Scared by the Bible* dares us to experience the horror present in the Bible's pages. Tracing the extra, the impossible, and the uncanny in stories familiar and foreign, Grafius shows that biblical horror is not a problem for theology but an opportunity. Sacred authors invited readers to grapple with their most visceral fears in order to see beyond the surface and reimagine the world that is and should be. This engaging and accessible book will delight fans of modern horror while furnishing fresh tools and insights for interpreting the Bible."

—*Anathea Portier-Young, associate professor of Old Testament at Duke Divinity School*

"Grafius has produced a body of work that makes him the biblical scholar in residence at the Last House on the Left. His new work sums up much of his scholarship for a popular reading audience, sure to be beloved by students and anyone interested in learning about this little known or understood side of scripture. You'll learn about the horror genre, but you'll also get a surprisingly witty and thoughtful introduction to how the pros do biblical scholarship. It's an amazing book and, once again, Grafius has shown he's on par with scholars like Bart Ehrmann and Elaine Pagels. . . if you could listen to the Cramps and Rob Zombie while reading them!"

—*W. Scott Poole, author of* Monsters in America *and* Dark Carnivals

"A deeply thoughtful and self-reflective invitation to explore the fascinating and disturbing terrain of biblical horror. Grafius understands that actually cracking open and reading the Bible raises more unsettling questions than it answers—questions about ourselves, about our social norms and conventions, and, for people of faith, about the biblical God. Required reading for anyone interested in biblical studies and/or horror studies."

—Timothy Beal, Florence Harkness professor of religion at Case Western University and author of Religion and Its Monsters

Scared by the Bible

The Roots of Horror in Scripture

Brandon R. Grafius

morehouse
PUBLISHING

Morehouse Publishing
19 East 34th Street New York, NY 10016
www.churchpublishing.org

Morehouse Publishing is an imprint of Church Publishing Incorporated.

Cover design by David Baldeosingh Rotstein
Typeset by Nord Compo

ISBN 978-1-64065-783-0 (paperback)
ISBN 978-1-64065-784-7 (eBook)

Library of Congress Control Number: 2025932441

Contents

Introduction Reading, Watching, and Feeling Horror 1

Section 1

Reading Horror (and the Bible) 23

One A (Ridiculously Brief) History of Horror 25

Two Monster Movies 47

Three What Is a Hermeneutics of Horror? 65

Section 2

Horror of the Self 79

Four Leviticus and the Flesh 81

Five Tales of Revenge 99

Section 3

Horror of the World 115

Six The People of the Land and the Horror of the Folk 117

Seven Demonic Forces at Work 137

Eight The Books of Kings, but Really the Books of War and Destruction 151

Section 4

Horror of the Divine 167

Nine Apocalypse Soon 169

Ten Ark Encounters at the Edge of the Universe 185

Conclusion Does the Bible Mean to Scare Us? 201

Appendix The Trauma (and Horror) of the Old Testament 211

Narrative Bibliography 219

Acknowledgments 245

Filmography 247

For Fenton and Reece,
little monsters no more.

". . . work out your own salvation
in fear and trembling."

Philippians 2:12 (KJV)

Introduction

Reading, Watching, and Feeling Horror

I was ten years old the first time I tried to read the Bible straight through, from cover to cover.

Not one of the children's Bibles I'd received in Sunday school, but an honest-to-God grown-up Bible. My grandmother, herself the widow of a Baptist minister, had given me a King James Version for my birthday. I'd already developed a self-image as a smart kid, I loved reading, and I had a bit of a stubborn streak that kicked in when adults told me I couldn't do something. All three of those combined to lead me on a rather quixotic quest to read through this tome, ten chapters a night, over the summer. The plan was solidified when I told my Sunday school teacher what I was thinking about doing, and she suggested that I might want to start with one of the Gospels first, since they were a little easier to get into.

Of course, she was absolutely right. There's hardly a better way to get people to question their faith than to have them sit down and read the Bible cover to cover, Genesis to Revelation. But there's also few better ways to get someone to plow ahead on a fool's errand than by telling them they should change their plan.

There's so much in the Bible that's strange to our modern ears (even if I had been reading a more contemporary translation). There's so much that doesn't seem to have anything to do with any of the elements of religion that we hear about as being the central components of our faith each Sunday at church. And there's so much of it that's off-putting, or that just feels wrong. Of course, I didn't know any of that as a ten-year-old—I just knew the kindly bearded guy who always seemed to be smiling while telling stories to the children on his lap.

In all honesty, the Bible's not a book for the squeamish, the faint of heart, or those looking to have their faith reassured. (At least not all of it.) It's full of passages that are strictly bound to its Near Eastern context of several thousand years ago. And it's full of places where God doesn't come across as looking like a very well-adjusted deity. In Sunday school, we all learned about the mean old Pharaoh's refusal to let Moses's people go—but most of us didn't learn that the reason Pharaoh refuses is that God "hardened his heart" so that God would have the chance to demonstrate his power through the series of plagues that fall upon Egypt. That first happens in Exodus 9:12; several previous times, Pharaoh hardens his own heart, or it just grows hard on its own, but here it's clearly stated that God does it. And then in 10:1, God confirms that he did this to Pharaoh so that he would have a chance to show off. With all of the first-born babies of Egypt as collateral damage.

Even at ten years old, I was feeling like the image of God as a grandfatherly old man in the clouds was naïve, but it still seemed a lot better than this vindictive, grouchy character that shows up in the Bible.

I made it through Genesis. There were enough great stories to get me through the begats, and enough places where I already had context from Sunday school that I could wade my way through the parts that didn't make sense. I knew the broad outlines of the Joseph story, although I didn't quite understand what was going on with Tamar and her father.

I even made it through Exodus, though the last half was more than a bit of an endurance test. I loved reading the original tales behind the Sunday school lessons and songs about letting the people go, and the plagues and the parting of the Red Sea were pretty cool. I wasn't quite sure why Moses went up to the mountaintop to talk with God about what to do with oxen that were repeat-goring offenders, or about the best way to treat your slaves. But I kept to my ten-chapters-a-night assignment. The nights started to feel a little longer around then.

It was when I got to Leviticus that my journey really crashed onto the rocks. I've learned since that this is a pretty common experience—I have yet to meet someone who made it through the legal codes of Leviticus and the seemingly pointless desert wanderings of Numbers the first time they tried to read the Bible straight through. But it was pretty galling for me as a young person; this was the faith I was being brought up in, a tradition that made so much sense to me when I learned about it in church. And here I get back to the foundational documents, and they weren't making a bit of sense. What did this book have to do with what we were doing in church every Sunday?

Part of it is a problem of expectations. We get the message from all around us that the Bible is supposed to be a source of eternal truths, and that the answers to all life's questions can be found in its pages. When I teach biblical interpretation, I often start by leading the students in a discussion about what the Bible means to them and how they understand it. More than once, I've had students respond with the slogan "Basic Instructions Before Leaving Earth." (This was also the title of a hip-hop song by Wu-Tang Clan founder GZA and affiliate Killah Priest; for me, it doesn't work as a song or as a bumper sticker.) Politicians who hold their Christianity as a key part of their public persona often traffic in this same kind of rhetoric. In an interview with Sean Hannity, Speaker of the House Mike Johnson told the host that if people wanted to know what he believed "about any issue under the sun" to just "go pick up a Bible off your shelf and read it." This would solve all questions.

But as Peter Enns has so eloquently pointed out, this type of answer involves a fundamental misunderstanding about what the Bible is and how it's supposed to function. The Bible has rules in it, sure—the Ten Commandments, the laws in Leviticus. But if it wasn't anything more than a list of do's and don'ts, I don't think we'd be paying any attention to it today. It would be sitting in a museum next to the Code of Hammurabi, an interesting cultural relic that could only tell us about the past.

Instead, the Bible is full of stories. It's full of prayers. It's full of poems and songs and pieces of history, and myths, and even some high-comedy satire. (Read the book of Jonah again if you don't believe that last part!) The Bible has all kinds of different styles of writing, different genres. Each of them has a different purpose and asks us to read them in a different way. If we treat the Bible like it's nothing but a set of rules, we're going to miss all the ways these different kinds of writing are attempting to communicate with us. The Bible doesn't work that way.

If we go diving into the book of Joshua seeking guidance for how we should think about certain issues, we're likely to be confused when all we find are stories featuring bloody battles. But if we recognize the kind of story it is, the narrative conventions it's working with, and how it tries to convey its messages, then we might have a chance to form a better understanding of how the Bible works. And to get there, we've got to learn to be better readers. One of the best ways to sharpen our reading skills—short of a whole bunch of practice, of course—is to do a little bit of thinking about genre.

The idea I'm really trying to introduce is a simple one. There are many different genres in the Bible. But there are only a handful of genres that we consider "good" or "Holy" enough to be a part of the Bible. Many of us have been brought up to believe that the Bible is good and holy, and as such must include only good and holy things in its writing. But, as I hope to demonstrate throughout the course of this book, our definitions of *good* and *holy* are far too small. Biblical scholar Steve Wiggins argues that, over the centuries, "the aura of sanctity . . . grew to surround Scripture" such that we didn't allow ourselves to see the horror threaded throughout its pages.

He continues: "This concept that the book itself was holy bore such theological weight that any recognition of the obvious—that the Bible contains much that qualifies as horror, as well as fiction—could not be properly addressed." If you stop and think about it, this proposition should be pretty uncontroversial. There's a lot of material in the Bible that, by any fair definition, would be most clearly categorized as horrific. And, as the pages to follow will explore, much of the book even adheres to some of the conventions that we've come to know as conventions of the horror genre.

I started my PhD program in Hebrew Bible with the idea of looking at the metaphors of the Bible, possibly working in the Psalms or the Prophets. But I remember the exact moment when I started wondering whether I could combine my love of horror with my study of the Bible. I was in a seminar on the history of Israel and doing some research on the Midianites. That led me to chapter 25 of the book of Numbers, where the Israelites are wandering in the desert and starting to have relationships with women from some of the other tribes they come into contact with. At one point, an Israelite man brings a Midianite woman into the camp, and they go off into a tent together. Moses doesn't know what to do, but the priest Phinehas—Aaron's grandson—picks up a spear and skewers them both. He's then praised for his great "zeal" for God. It's a horrific enough scene on its own, but the synapse that fired in my brain was that I'd seen this exact death scene before, in *Friday the 13th, Part 2.* (I'm a little embarrassed to admit to knowing that!) It made me realize two things: 1) Maybe the Bible itself intends to horrify its readers; and 2) Maybe we should take what we know about interpreting horror and use it to read some of these passages?

Understanding Horror as a Genre

Throughout this book, I'll keep returning to these questions: What is this story trying to scare you with? And how is it trying to scare you? If we can answer these two questions, we might get at something that at least looks like an answer to another question: What does it mean? How does this story understand the universe? (Or—when we make a transition to religious horror—the divine.)

So we'll look at Bible stories that seem to be next-door neighbors to monster movies. And Bible stories that look an awful lot like folk horror, or that share some family resemblance to revenge films. Throughout all these explorations, we'll bounce back and forth between Bible stories and film to isolate one key recurring insight: some of the most troubling Bible stories have some gears that turn in a way that's similar to contemporary horror movies (even if we acknowledge the vast gulf between these forms). If we understand how these horror movies work, we might gain some insights to carry back with us into the biblical text. The first step is to acknowledge that some of the texts in the Bible are horror stories—that's an important hurdle to get over. But once we've leaped over that one, there's another challenge looming: How do we read horror? How do we take these stories and unpack them to figure out what they're trying to tell us about what scares us? Because I truly believe—as I think many of the biblical writers did—that if we understand what scares us, we also understand what's important to us. If we understand what we're afraid of, we understand what matters to us.

To get to the heart of these questions, we've got to start developing a hermeneutics of horror. I want to be a little careful here; I'm not trying to say that the Bible is an ancient form of a Stephen King novel. But I do think that there are a number of passages that have a number of features we can recognize as participating in the genre of horror.

We use genres all the time. They help us to understand things like fairy tales and mystery novels, but they're not just about pieces of literature. When you go into a restaurant, you know that the large piece of laminated paper in front of you that has a lengthy list of food items is telling you what the kitchen will be able to serve you—and that the dollar amount next to it indicates the price they will charge for this item. You're able to do this because you recognize it as a menu, and you understand "menu" as a genre, with certain expectations, certain goals, and certain ways of conveying information.

And of course, we talk about genre all the time in the entertainment we consume, whether it's books, music, or movies. We know how to distinguish a country song from a hip-hop track—and because we know those two genres well enough, we can enjoy when something comes along like "Old Town Road" and mashes the two of them together in ways we might not expect. Generally, we know what to expect when we sit down and listen to a radio station, because they'll mostly play songs from within a small group of different genres. The radio station won't surprise us too much by playing a song that sounds completely different from what came before it.

Genre is a strong enough identifier for movies that we usually group them together by genre, whether it was in the video stores of days past or on streaming services today. There are separate sections for drama, horror, comedy, and action, among many others. These categorizations help us know what to expect and give us a clue about whether the movie we're considering is what we're looking for on a given evening.

One of the main markers of genre in movies, as in books, is narrative structure, the kind of conflicts, plot points, and even resolutions you can expect to find. In a romance, you'll expect to see a couple who seems like they might be a good romantic fit—to the audience, if not initially to the characters themselves. The plot will center around the obstacles that get thrown up in the way of their eventual marriage, whether that's another interested party, a series of missed connections, or rival families. By the end, we expect these obstacles will have been overcome, and the couple will be able to live happily ever after. In action movies, we can expect to see a villain who develops a plot to enrich himself at the expense of others, and a hero who's the only one who can stand in the way. We'll expect to see a climactic battle and the hero triumphing over seemingly impossible odds.

But narrative isn't the only thing that helps us recognize genre. Sometimes, an even more important marker is how the story tries to make us feel. If we're not laughing, it's probably not a comedy. If we don't have a rush of adrenaline, followed by some sense of catharsis at the conclusion, we're probably not watching an action movie. (Or at least we're not watching a very successful comedy or action film—if those movies don't make us feel that way, they might just be poor examples of the genre, or at least one that isn't working for us.) And if we're feeling choked up at the end of a play or a film because everything has gone wrong for our hero and heroine, we're probably watching a tragedy. As much as what happens, the attempt to engage the audience emotionally, with a particular affect in mind, is central to how genres work.

And horror is all about how it makes the audience feel. Scholar Adam Charles Hart has gone as far as to suggest that, at its core, horror doesn't need to be a narrative genre at all—what's most important is the "centrality of the sensational address," the way in which horror tries to fill us with dread. Horror is the genre that most directly hits us right in the feels. We're seeing a rush of horror movies right now that are really exploring what this means—movies like *The Outwater*, which takes the found footage genre and twists the structures of space and time until we're hardly able to tell up from down, or like *Skinamarink*, which features just about no plot aside from a pair of young children trapped in a house, but spends its entire running time trying to drill down into our deepest sense of growing unease and discomfort.

Of course, *how* horror instills these emotions in us ranges widely from film to film. The way a movie in the *Saw* franchise makes us squirm with fear is very different from the slow-building dread we experience from a film like *The Witch.* But in both, the narrative tries to generate a pretty intense response. Just like you can't have a comedy that doesn't at least try to make its audience laugh, you can't have a horror movie that doesn't, in one way or another, try to scare us. Or at least unsettle us.

One of the things we'll pay attention to in the chapters to follow is what *kind* of horror story we're reading in the Bible—because as even this brief overview reminds us, horror isn't all the same. It doesn't all work in the same way, it doesn't try to fill us with fear or dread using the same set of tools. The clearer we can be about what kind of story or poem we're reading, and what that tells us about what it might be trying to do, the better our chances are of producing a reading that's meaningful.

For me, one of the most interesting thinkers of genre is the Russian theorist Mikhail Bakhtin. He was writing primarily in the early and mid-twentieth century, always trying to stay one step ahead of the totalitarian state in which he found himself living.

For Bakhtin, genre wasn't even primarily about literature or art—it was about constructing a worldview. Genres have a particular way of speaking about the world, and things they try to convey about the world. You might think of a genre like the 1940s *film noir*, with its rain-soaked alleyways, elaborate shadows, and morally ambiguous detective characters who end up being undone by a *femme fatale.* While the plot points help us to group these movies together, and the style might be an even bigger marker, what binds them together is the worldview they present. In this world, the easy morality that we might be used to in novels and cinema is revealed as naïve, and we're instead presented with a world full of fallen people struggling to make choices when all they're presented with are bad options. The world is a deck that's stacked against us, whoever we might be, and there's no good way out of these dark alleys. Even films noirs where the protagonist makes it out alive at the end—a movie like *The Maltese Falcon*, perhaps—end with the realization that all the struggle we've just witnessed was toward a meaningless end. Instead of good triumphing over evil, the story confirms that everything is shadow. It's the same kind of cosmic loneliness that we find in some of Paul's letters and the stories of H. P. Lovecraft.

Reading Outcomes in Horror

While we usually know a horror movie when we see one, figuring out exactly how it's working—and what, precisely, it's telling us about the world around us—can be a trickier matter. As a genre, horror is inherently puckish. It's always subverting itself, setting up traditions just so the next movie can undermine them, and reconfiguring what the rules are. Horror is an unstable place to be.

Part of the challenge is that outcomes aren't necessarily moral evaluations the way they are in many other narrative genres. Here's what I mean by that: In a comedy, the main characters end up happy at the end. (For comedies that follow Shakespeare's template, they usually end up getting married.) If characters end up in a bad spot, or have their plans thwarted, we can tell that we're not supposed to side with them. The comedy has rejected their way of being in the world in favor of the moral worldview of the heroes. The heroes present to us how the narrative wishes the world was and how we're supposed to act in our own lives. It's the same thing with an action movie—heroes get good outcomes, villains get bad ones. We can tell who's side the movie is on because they end up succeeding in the end.

But with horror, you can't always tell this. Sometimes, a character meets a bad end because their way of being in the world is rejected by the narrative—perhaps they were greedy, or selfish in some other way, such that the unfortunate consequences they're suffering are just desserts. For this kind of horror, think of the *Tales from the Crypt* comics and the HBO series that adapted some of its tales in the 1990s. These stories involve characters who do something awful (or are just awful people), who then experience a supernatural comeuppance that's poetically connected to their sins. As we will see, the Bible has stories like this too.

And it might be as simple as that the characters are just too curious! A number of these stories seem to be written to illustrate the maxim that it's best to let sleeping dogs lie. M. R. James even titled one of his most famous ghost stories "A Warning to the Curious." The canon of horror is rife with characters who might have lived to see the dawn if they'd resisted the urge to see what was in that tomb, or what was causing that strange noise they heard outside. More than being rebellious, it makes me wonder if curiosity was what pushed Adam and Eve to take a bite of the fruit.

When you run into a story like this, it's clear that these characters are being introduced because their values are likely to be rejected—both by the narrative and by the viewers. The horror story is using them as a cautionary tale, establishing a worldview that rejects the moral system of these characters. When they get what's coming to them, all is right with the world again.

But that's not how all horror stories work. Often, characters that we admire meet grisly ends. Sometimes it's even minor characters who just put up a great fight before finally succumbing to the monster or serial killer. We admire those characters, and their deaths strike us as an injustice—a confirmation that whatever force they struggled against was truly a force of evil. So instead of being presented with an enriching moral example, we're presented with a sobering illustration of the dark and inescapable forces at work in the world. Sometimes, there can be no good outcome, no matter how good you are, because you're living in a world that's governed by the rules of horror.

It all comes down to a simple paradox, one that viewers always have to contend with in the genre of horror: Horror can both present to us the world as it should be, but threatened by forces that would seek to unravel it; or present to us a nightmarish version of the world as it is, but not as it should be.

Genre and Expectations

One of the main arguments of this book is that to become better readers of the Bible, we have to become better readers of horror. That's because the Bible contains many, many stories, poems, and other types of literature that, in some way or another, connect with the genre of horror. It might be that the narrative is straight out of a monster movie. Or it might just be that the imagery asks us to imagine a horrifying situation, putting ourselves as readers in a position where we're asked to envision ourselves fighting Leviathan, or experience what it must feel like to be in the grave. When we know how to read horror, we'll be able to better approach these passages and see what they might be trying to tell us as readers—and as people of faith.

More and more, scholars have come to view genre as being less about the book or the movie itself—genre isn't something that a movie *is,* or even *has,* because it checks off a certain number of boxes. Genre is a tool that audiences and cultures create as a way to talk about and receive works of literature, or movies, or whatever it may be. Genres help us to know how to take in what we're looking at, and to process it.

One way of looking at the problem so many readers have with the Bible is that it's a mismatch of genres. We have all these ideas in our mind about what "The Bible" is—I would suggest it's its own genre, the genre of "Bible." Except, this genre that we have in our minds isn't a genre that exists, and it certainly isn't the genre that the actually-existing-Bible-as-it's-written participates in. It might be that we get this genre fixed in our minds from the children's Bibles we read, or have read to us before we're able to read, or from what we learn in Sunday school and other church activities from when we're young. Or it might just be that it's the cultural water we're swimming in. In our minds, this Bible features stories that are morally uplifting, have an easy-to-digest message, and are clearly applicable to our lives today.

Of course, this idea of the Bible, this imagined genre, doesn't survive very much contact with the actual Bible. It's certainly possible to pull out enough passages to create a cut-and-paste version of the Bible that matches these expectations, but any attempt to read it through from Genesis to Revelation quickly reveals that it's a very different book than this idea we have in our heads. We're not reading what we expected to be reading, so we don't really know what to do with it.

That's the conundrum that my ten-year-old self faced when I first tried to read the Bible straight through, and the conundrum that many readers face anew all the time. There's one easy solution: Don't read the Bible, and just receive it as the imaginary book you learned about as a child. I've heard this solution described as being similar to how we treat the software agreements we're confronted with every time we install a new program on our computer: We don't read it, but just click "I Agree" and assume that whatever's in it is fine.

The problem with that is that it only allows for a surface-level engagement with the book, and with all of the religious heritage that has stemmed from it. To truly dive more deeply into the Christian faith, we've got to start by accepting this book as it is, not as the Sunday school fantasy we might wish it was.

Instead, it's a book filled with horrors—often juxtaposed uncomfortably with the grace and love that we've come to expect from the Bible. This book will help us unpack that idea by first giving a very brief overview of the history of horror so we can have some idea of how the Bible fits in. We'll talk a little about monsters, and then back up to introduce some more questions of how we read and interpret. After that, the next three sections will all be about the kinds of things the Bible tries to make us afraid of: afraid for our own lives, afraid for our communities and world, and afraid for the cosmos. Hopefully, we can keep one eye on what it's trying to convey by making us afraid of these things. The Bible isn't just trying to scare us for fun, and I think it's a deeper question than just trying to scare us into good behavior. It's trying to reshape how we think about the world, the universe, and God.

In order to help us think through these questions and try to organize them in a way that makes sense, I've tried to organize chapters together that center around similar questions of where this fear is located—and the broad topic that the narrative pushes us to think about. Horror, as a genre, can be roughly divided into three major areas of concern: the individual, the society, and the universe. I think we can find this same set of concerns within the Bible itself, perhaps with the divine standing in for the universe.

Timothy Beal, in the second edition of his seminal book *Religion and Its Monsters*, argues that monsters are designed to disturb any of these spaces, or perhaps all three at once: "[T]he monster is that which invades personal, social, and/or cosmic order and security, disturbing one's sense of at-homeness in oneself, one's society, and one's world," he summarizes. Horror is what happens when these areas are threatened, questioned, or exposed as being less stable than we thought. Sometimes the purpose of horror is to put the fractured pieces of security back together, and other times it's designed to leave us with the lingering sense of discomfort at the state of the world we live in. Like contemporary horror, the Bible uses horror for both of these effects as well.

As Beal's quote makes plain, these distinctions aren't sharp and clear; often, horror will function on multiple levels at the same time—sometimes all three. It's not like a story that's about an individual doesn't also concern itself with society or the universe, if only because part of what concerns us as individuals is our proper place within these larger spheres. These concerns are all blended together, mixed up and tangled around one another. But more often than not, a horror narrative will lift up one of these concerns as primary, with the others moving more or less into the background.

Think about a movie like *Halloween*, where Michael Myers chases babysitter Laurie Strode through the peaceful Haddonfield suburbs. While there's plenty of sociological subtext, our primary fear as viewers is for Laurie's life and how she's going to get away from this masked killer. There's clearly more going on there—I've written about slashers as being a product of the Reagan revolution elsewhere—but the fear that's presented directly to us is just for the safety of this young woman.

But then there's a movie like *The Purge*, in which a dystopian version of our country celebrates an annual holiday during which all laws are suspended. We're following the home invasion of a singular family, but the film keeps returning us to concern for society as a whole; this family is a microcosm of our larger social relations. Particularly as the series moves on and we learn more and more about the politics behind the Purge, our fears become less about individual characters and more about what this says about the world this movie is presenting—and how it connects with our own world.

And finally, we have horror narratives where the concern is even bigger than our world. It could be cosmic horror, like the Nicolas Cage–led adaptation of H. P. Lovecraft's story *The Color Out of Space*, or a religious-themed horror movie like *The Seventh Sign.* But in these movies, we're moving even farther away from the individual, and even away from an analysis of contemporary society, to ruminations about how the universe works, and about the divine (or otherwise) beings who are managing everything behind the scenes.

It's not a perfect schema—there are obviously movies and stories that are tough to put in one of these categories, places where there's slippage from one to the next, and all sorts of cases on the margins that cause problems. But I still think it's a helpful organizational tool, one that lets us sift through the different kinds of horror in a way that can provide some insight into our relationship with the stories. We began this book with monsters as a general introduction to horror, and because it's such an obvious link with the Bible. But from there, we focus on individuals, then society, and finally the cosmos and the divine. Hopefully, it's a structure that seems intuitive, and also helps to make some sense out of all the weird and terrifying stories that we're going to explore.

Once we've made these leaps, we can begin to explore how much more richness, more complexity, more life, there is in the book as it actually exists than in the safer, sanitized version we have in our heads. Once we've made that leap, we're ready to explore the Bible on a much deeper level and to really, truly, start reading it. You might even find that this approach can get you through Leviticus and Numbers, and into the books beyond.

Section 1

Reading Horror (and the Bible)

1 A (Ridiculously Brief) History of Horror

Friday Night and Sunday Morning

I grew up in the 1980s and 1990s, an era where we moved from cable television to VHS tapes to DVDs. When I was young, movies were on HBO. My friends and I used to joke that the initials actually stood for "Hey, *Beastmaster*'s On!" because that stupid movie seemed to be on at least five times a week, but it was hard to complain about the cornucopia that beamed through our TV each month. Where my movie watching really took off was in high school, when I started to have enough independence that I could get to the video store on my own. I could bike to the grocery store down the street from me, which had a whole roomful of video rentals. My mind was blown even more when I finally got to an honest-to-goodness independent video store.

I wasn't a loner in my high school days, but I was definitely an introvert. A lot of days, I would bike home from school and spend the afternoon listening to CDs, trying to write a poem or two, and maybe practicing some music. I played bass for an aspiring rock band (a friend described us as a cross between Faith No More and U2, which was awfully generous, and probably not particularly fair to either of those bands) and sang in the school choir. But there were two days a week when I was most consistently in a group of people: Friday night and Sunday morning.

Sunday morning was church. I sang in the choir, made mischief in the youth group, and tried to put my adult face on when the congregation invited me to serve as the youth representative for the Board of Deacons. I wrestled with questions of what I believed about God and faith, like just about everyone does. At the same time, I always felt that I could bring my whole self with me to church on Sunday morning, and leave feeling as if I might be able to get through the next week.

And Friday night was movie night, preferably with as many friends as I could pull together. I hosted a few Bad Film Festivals, trying my best to emulate the vibe of *Mystery Science Theater 3000.* These events were complete with score cards, with friends gathered together to laugh at some truly terrible examples of cinema. On the first evening, the *Conan the Barbarian*–wannabe movie *Ator the Fighting Eagle* barely beat out the Vanilla Ice vehicle *Cool as Ice.* (The competition was stiff—it was tough to overcome Vanilla Ice's immortal line, "Yo babe, drop the zero, and get with the hero.") Everyone rated them in categories including unoriginality, bad acting, poor taste, and general incompetence; then I tabulated all of the scores and came up with the official winner. Those were good times—movies that spectacularly awful can only be enjoyed in a company of like-minded goofballs, everyone joining in the spirit of mirth to poke fun.

But where I really found myself wanting to be around others wasn't for comedically terrible films—it was for movies that were truly terrifying. From my teenage years on, I've shared this in common with lots of people. I love scary movies, and I love them even more when they can be shared together.

Looking back on those years, it makes sense that watching horror movies and going to church were two spaces where I wanted community. As we'll explore throughout this book, they're both spaces where the major questions of life get explored, where we have the chance to work out (with fear and trembling) what all of this means. Sometimes, that process is too terrifying to undertake alone. So we do it with our community, whether that's in church or watching movies on a Friday night.

In this book, I hope to explore some of the ways that horror and religion are tangled together. To start, we'll talk about how these two spaces—horror and religion—have been bound together from the earliest days, from when we first started telling stories and when we first started thinking about God. So I'll give a brief (brief!) overview of horror movies and stories, and then show how these narrative forms have their roots in ancient religious texts.

Horror in the Multiplex

The history of horror cinema is wrapped up with the history of film itself. As soon as people started to explore how they could use this new medium to tell stories, they started exploring how it could be used to evoke fear. One of Thomas Edison's earliest experiments with film was a version of *Frankenstein*, lasting all of sixteen minutes. Even before that, the French pioneer Georges Méliès directed a number of films with skeletons and haunted houses in the late eighteen and early nineteen hundreds, many running under five minutes in length. Famously, one of the first films ever shown publicly was a single shot of a train approaching the screen, which purportedly left audiences terrified at the image of this steel behemoth hurtling toward them. We would hardly think of this as a horror movie today. But for its original audience, who had no idea how to process a two-dimensional image that seemed to be barreling directly toward them and preparing to break through the thin screen at the front of the theater, it was terrifying.

Perhaps the most influential cycle of horror films from this era came out of Germany, in what's come to be known as the style of Expressionism. Films like *The Cabinet of Dr. Caligari* and the original *Nosferatu* were full of outlandish sets with unnatural angles that looked like they walked straight out of a fever dream. At least as terrifying as the figure of *Nosferatu*'s Count Orlok was his shadow, with unbelievably long fingernails that stretched up and around the curved staircase. These images would have an enormous impact on the later films noirs, as well as on more contemporary American horror. These movies look a lot more like what we would expect from a horror movie today, even if they're still dated. But they clearly connect with the *fin de siècle* Gothic novels that were en vogue at the time, from authors such as Bram Stoker and Arthur Machen, and cast an Orlok-sized shadow over the rest of horror film history.

But as Kendall Phillips discusses in his masterful exploration of the development of the horror film *A Place of Darkness*, the description of early silent films as "horror" was a late arriver on the scene. At first, these films were marketed as being "shocking," or "thrilling." It wasn't until the 1930s that the term *horror* started to appear on movie posters and in newspaper ads.

By whatever name they may have been called, there were a number of horror films in the silent era originating in America, as well as being imported from overseas. Lon Chaney chilled audiences with his portrayal of the Phantom of the Opera, and the Old Dark House genre had its birth with films like *The Cat and the Canary* in 1927. Usually, the horror wasn't supernatural in nature—the old dark house wasn't haunted, but there was a malevolent relative trying to scare everyone away so that he would inherit the family's fortune all to himself. Russian theorist Tzvetan Todorov would refer to this as the uncanny (in a nod to Sigmund Freud, whose essay "The

Uncanny" is one of the founding pieces of horror criticism), where things that seem to be supernatural in origin end up having a rational explanation. People who were kids in the 1970s and 1980s probably think of it as the Scooby-Doo model, where no matter what kind of spookiness happens on screen, you know that Old Man Withers is going to have his mask pulled off before the half hour's up. There was also a heavy dose of comedy in these early horror films. We think of horror-comedy as a special subgenre, with entries like *The Evil Dead 2* or *Tucker and Dale vs. Evil*, but it's a combination with a long pedigree.

Comedy starts to take a back seat in what's often regarded as the first golden age of horror films, starting with the mammoth success of Universal Studios' *Dracula* in 1931. By the time the year was out, the studio had rushed an adaptation of *Frankenstein* into the theaters—and introduced *horror* into the generic lexicon. The 1930s were when we first saw monsters flourish on screen, with Universal cranking out sequels to their smash hits and launching new franchises like *The Mummy*, and other studios trying to build their own horror portfolio with adaptations of Edgar Allan Poe stories and other horrifying projects. It was also the Great Depression, and there were early rumblings of war in Europe, when much of the world felt an ever-increasing anxiety over the state of current affairs. Scholars have noted a consistent pattern: throughout the twentieth century, horror becomes more popular as social anxiety rises. It seems a clear confirmation that horror is, in fact, one of the places we go to process the worries of our more mundane lives.

Many consider the 1950s to be another decade of horror, as the science-fiction films that dominated drive-in theaters were really horror movies with aliens instead of blood-sucking vampires. (And these movies reflected their age's anxieties as well—notice how many of them have nuclear weapons barely hidden in the background.) But for most scholars, the modern horror film starts in 1968, with the launch of *Night of the Living Dead* and *Rosemary's Baby.* There were some forerunners—certainly Alfred Hitchcock's *Psycho*, maybe the Hammer films out of the United Kingdom if you think of them as being more than updated Universal horror films—but 1968 was the year when these outliers moved into the center. In *Night*, the movie that sets the template for every zombie apocalypse movie since, people aren't heroic, there's no happy ending, and the monsters are our neighbors. It's a far cry from stories like *Dracula*, where the monster comes from overseas and we have to protect our community from the foreign threat. And in *Rosemary's Baby*, the titular character finds herself the victim of a satanic conspiracy, with her husband and fellow apartment tenants at the center.

These two movies helped to establish the palette that horror movies still work from today. Horror might come from without, from aliens or a country across the sea, but it's at least as likely to come from within (whether "within" signifies our communities, our families, or even our own bodies). And while the monster always threatens what's normal, it isn't a given that "normal" is good, or that we want to return to it. Interestingly, we'll see in some of the explorations to follow that this is frequently how the Bible uses horror as well—to poke holes in our idea of "normal," to help us see that how we understand the world is far too small.

Another History: Horror in Religion

The previous section told a ridiculously abbreviated version of the history of the horror film. Add in its roots in Gothic literature of the eighteenth century, in books like Horace Walpole's *The Castle of Otranto* and or Ann Radcliffe's *The Mysteries of Odolpho*, draw the line from them to Poe in the nineteenth century and the spiritualist movement that saw a society-wide obsession with talking to ghostly spirits, and you'd have something like a conventional scholarly approach to the horror genre. But that overlooks so much horror that came before, and ignores the field in which horror has been most prominent in the pre-modern age: the field of religion.

For some scholars, stories about monsters and other dangers of the dark are as old as storytelling and served the primary function of warning us about how to stay alive in dangerous times. Scholar Paul Trout, for example, suggests that myths evolved out of our experience of being the prey of dangerous, overwhelmingly powerful predators—and that these myths contain the collected wisdom of survivors who have avoided becoming meat. While this theory offers an evolutionary portrait of how horror developed, its answer as to why we like horror stories is actually very similar to that of contemporary cognitive psychologists, such as Mathias Clasen. Clasen, like Trout, argues that we're drawn to horror stories because they help prepare us for what to do in dangerous situations. We get to see dangerous situations acted out from the comfort of our own living rooms, and to explore how infrequently it works to respond to an intruder in the house by running upstairs instead of out the front door. We spend the movie thinking through what we might do in a similar situation and begin to develop plans of both escape and attack. In essence, horror movies serve as survival training for our minds so that we'll be ready to react to any dangerous situation we might face in real life.

There's some sense in what these scholars suggest; it seems logical that we'd be drawn to the ability to enhance our chances of survival from a safe vantage point. But I don't think it explains why monsters and other types of horror show up so frequently in religious texts—after all, those texts aren't primarily about how to avoid being eaten. In many religious traditions, including my own background of Protestant Christianity, survival is actually thought of as less important than more eternal matters. We need only think of Jesus's well-known words to his disciples in Luke 9:24–25: "For those who want to save their life will lose it, and those who lose their life for my sake will save it. What does it profit them if they gain the whole world, but lose or forfeit themselves?" Clearly, Jesus isn't interested in giving instructions for hiding from sabretooth tigers.

Horror isn't about instructions; it's about stories and images. Darryl Jones presses far beyond the early silent films or Gothic novels to find the origins of horror in ancient religious texts; in speaking of ghosts, he notes that both ghosts and "horror more generally" are "intrinsic to civilization." And biblical scholar Steve Wiggins has traced "horror back to the Bible" and even older religious texts from the Ancient Near East. He summarizes: "The classification of the Bible as 'nonfiction' has prevented it from rightfully being considered as containing the early roots of horror . . . the backstory of horror fits quite easily at the origins of the Western literary tradition." As we shall see, it's not just that horror is found in the Bible—it's that many of the specific *types* of horror stories that are familiar to us today have clear antecedents in the biblical text (as well as in the texts and traditions of many other religions).

Horror then is not alien to our religious traditions, but rather a deeply component part of them. To summarize, we've strung together a series of observations: 1) It seems plausible that part of the purpose of horror stories is as a sort of survival training; 2) Religious traditions, broadly speaking, are not overly concerned with this type of survival of the body; but, 3) There is a strong element of horror found across a wide range of religions, and this mode is represented very strongly within the Bible. This tells me that the exploration of dangerous situations and training for how to survive them might be part of the purpose of horror, but it can't be the sole purpose—and maybe not even the primary one. The primary reason for the Bible's use of horror instead seems more linked to the realm of theology. It's less about how we save ourselves from danger, and more about how we enlarge our understanding of God and the world.

Properly Human Questions

In her fascinating book *The Secret Life of Puppets*, scholar Victoria Nelson argues that popular culture has become more and more fascinated with the kinds of questions that used to be thought of as "religious" questions as the world has become more secular. These are questions that we all have and that need an outlet—if religion no longer offers that outlet, then the questions will migrate into our popular entertainment. "Consuming art forms of the fantastic," she writes in the book's preface, "is only one way that we as nonbelievers allow ourselves, unconsciously, to believe." It's a fascinating point, and one that strikes me as deeply true—with one huge caveat. Popular culture's exploration of religious questions isn't something that's just started to happen as people stopped going to church every Sunday morning. It's been happening as long as there's been popular culture—and in the stories, poems, and songs that have existed since humans first became storytellers.

Scholar of religion Douglas Cowan has argued that questions about the meaning of life, about suffering, about the nature of the world, aren't really religious questions. He writes: "Although, by cultural convention and social dominance, we have tended to label these kind of questions *religious*, they are not . . . these are all *properly human questions.*" These are questions we all ask because we are fundamentally meaning-making creatures. But while the spaces of religion are natural places for us to ask them, Sunday morning doesn't have a monopoly. We continue asking these questions throughout the week, so it's perfectly natural that they'd show up in all sorts of places—including the movies we watch and the books we read.

I've argued elsewhere that horror is one of the best modes through which to explore these questions. Having characters faced with death, often by ghosts or monsters who force us to question the boundaries of what we thought we knew about the world, is a natural canvas on which to paint questions about what this all means. These monsters, these dread-filled narratives, shadowy corners, and undead pasts returning to haunt the present, are natural ways to express religious ideas and push us to think outside of the mundane world that we're accustomed to.

One of the main propositions of this book is that the Bible is filled with horror, but that the horror is of a number of different varieties. And that each type of horror asks us to read it in a different way and tries to get at a different set of questions and explorations about the world. *Godzilla* doesn't communicate in the same way as *The Sixth Sense*, and neither of these movies communicate the same way as does *Friday the 13th*. In short, by becoming better readers of horror—more attuned to these generic conventions, more open to the particular forms and ways of communicating that each genre of horror has—we can also become better readers of the Bible.

Jacob at the Riverbank

We will never know if ancient Israelites gathered around a fire late at night to tell each other stories. Whatever campfire rituals they had certainly look different from the roasted hot dogs and adult beverages that we've become accustomed to. But if we were to translate one of the stories from Genesis into a campfire tale, a story meant to send a shiver down everyone's spine and make the night sky feel just a little bit darker, it might sound something like this:

> *He wasn't sure why he had sent his servants on ahead. Not the ones he had sent to meet his brother; sending them ahead was perfectly understandable, rational even. Who knew—the gifts he sent them with might calm Esau enough to give Jacob a chance to talk his way out of this mess, right? And if not, the goods he sent with them wouldn't matter to Jacob anyway. Sending these servants on ahead*

was an obvious choice, even if Jacob felt little hope that the ploy would work.

What he wasn't sure of was why he had decided to stay behind and send the rest of his servants across the river, carrying Jacob's tents and everything else he owned in the world that he wasn't offering up to Esau in tribute. He sent his servants and all of these things on ahead of him, across the river, telling them he'd catch up with them tomorrow. He could see the confusion in his servants' eyes as they received these commands, but they went ahead without questioning. They'd seen their master's behavior become increasingly odd and inscrutable over the last few weeks. This just seemed like one more step along a path they couldn't see, but could only follow.

And even more than his servants, Jacob didn't understand why he had sent his family away. Both of his wives, their maids, and all eleven children—he asked them to go with these servants, crossing the river on their own, promising to meet them the next day. For some reason, Jacob needed to be alone this night. The land was silent, only the gentle burbling of the creek beside him to remind him that time was continuing to move. The stars shone overhead, and Jacob occasionally glanced up at them, thinking about how many of them there were, and how small his family was, in spite of the promise that had been given to Abraham.

He heard something up ahead, a scratching that crackled through the flowing water. It made him squint his eyes at the darkness ahead of him, and he thought he could see something moving among the scraggly brush that lined the riverbank. There was something ahead of him. A desert animal, perhaps, on a nocturnal hunt for prey? But before Jacob could fix his eyes on it or wonder further what it might be, it was alongside of him, rough hands grabbing his shoulder and dragging him into the river. The crisp water ran up to his knees, but he hardly had time to feel the cold before he felt this stranger's leg behind his, forcing him backward and tumbling into the water. Jacob held on, taking the stranger down with him. Jacob held on.

This is one of my favorite horror stories of the Bible. If you're a lifelong church-goer, like I am, you've probably read or heard it many times. But you might not have thought of it as a horror story before. The retelling you just read doesn't change anything in the text, or even add anything new, other than some atmospheric descriptions that emphasize what's already there. But hopefully it helps you see the point clearly: at its heart, this is a horror story.

This encounter of Genesis 32:24–32, between Jacob and a divine being—an angel, or perhaps even God—is one of the strangest in all of the Bible. Jacob is in a difficult spot, with his long-running feud with his brother Esau about to come to a head. (Jacob wasn't very nice to Esau throughout their childhood, culminating in him tricking his not-so-bright brother into handing over his inheritance to Jacob in exchange for a bowl of soup.) Jacob and his family have been on the run from Esau, but it seems like Jacob's gotten to the end of the line. He's received word that Esau is coming to meet him with four hundred men, and the best plan Jacob's got is to send some presents ahead and hope that Esau looks kindly on him. As far as plans go, it's not a great one.

In the middle of all this, Jacob finds himself walking alone at night. He's sent his family across the river Jabbuk ahead of him, and Jacob takes an evening stroll along the banks. As many of us know from watching horror movies, walking alone at night is a good way to get yourself in trouble. And horrifying events are always more likely to happen during times of stress and deep self-reflection—ghosts, monsters, and all sorts of nefarious creatures seem to be attracted to our dark nights of the soul. (Think about how many haunted house stories start with a family struggling to stay together, perhaps either wrestling with grief or questions of divorce, and terrified about their finances.) Jacob finds this out when he runs into a man standing along the riverbank.

The biblical narrative style is famously laconic; that reaches one of its apexes here, where the text simply says, "Jacob was left alone; and a man wrestled with him until daybreak" (32:24). That's it—there's no further introduction, no sense of how Jacob responded, no sense of what the man looked like, or anything. It's all left up to our imagination. And as a reader, I sure have plenty of questions: Did this man say anything to Jacob, or did he just start attacking?

Did Jacob agree to this wrestling match, or did he try to talk his way out of it first? Was it set up as a friendly match, or was Jacob worried that this man might be trying to kill him? There are so many gaps in this text, so many questions that are fundamentally unanswerable.

And the questions don't really get answered throughout the story. Jacob and this being wrestle, Jacob refuses to let go until he receives a blessing, and eventually the blessing comes—in the form of both a new name ("Israel") and a permanent limp. Jacob managed to wrestle this divine being to a draw and received both a blessing and a wounding. But he greets the morning with a new sense of hope, and things end up working out well between him and Esau.

Along with all these unanswered questions, reading the passage also produces an emotional response. Here, I'm going to try to be careful—while I imagine that many of you will have a similar response, emotional responses are also in some ways always unique.

I realize that one of the primary emotions this passage engenders is disorientation; not necessarily confusion, because we can envision the main pieces of the action. It's the edges that get blurry and make me feel like I don't know quite where I am. I'm also disoriented because of the expectations I bring to the text. While I've spent over a decade studying and teaching the less-than-savory passages of the Bible, I can't quite shake my Sunday school feelings that tell me this is supposed to be a text of comfort and joy—because all texts of the Bible are, necessarily, about comfort and joy. And instead, we get a threatening nighttime environment and a deity or angel who wants to fight.

There's a standard interpretation of this passage, of course. Jacob wrestles with the divine, and is gifted the new name of Israel, which seems to mean "Wrestles with God." So Israel's very vocation is to do this kind of struggling with the divine, receiving blessings that come at a cost that we pay from our own bodies. The life of faith is an act of wrestling, one that can be frightening at times but always works out for the best. And while we might wrestle with God, God will always bless us in the end.

I know this, and it's a great interpretation of the passage. But for me, it also leaves out how the passage makes me feel; it rushes to the blessing and downplays the horror of living through this struggle. Besides, couldn't the Bible have made this point without making us witness this life-or-death confrontation? Couldn't we find a more peaceful way to make the point that the life of faith can feel like wrestling? Couldn't we get to this conclusion without being made to feel afraid?

But as I write this, I realize I've also pointed the way toward some further clarity in that last question. The life of faith can feel like wrestling, yes. So in this text, we're given the opportunity to feel that for ourselves. We feel the horror that Jacob experienced, the horror that pushed him toward a new understanding of himself and God.

So Jacob feels horror at this encounter with the divine being, and we experience it along with him. It's a horror borne of the setting, borne of the tension of the wrestling act, borne of the disorientating nature of the passage. We feel the horror that Jacob feels. And Jacob is able to use that experience of horror to learn something—the emotion is generative. Like Jacob, we feel something so that we can learn something.

This connection makes me circle back to the disorientation that I identified earlier. Disorientation is one of the key affects that horror frequently produces, often in conjunction with other emotions. When we feel disoriented, we're unsettled, we're nervous, we're on edge. Think about how often a horror movie will show us a camera angle that seems off—maybe tilted to one side, or maybe through a fish eye lens like those horrifying hallways of the 1960 version of *The Haunting.* Or maybe it's clearly a camera that's supposed to represent a point-of-view shot, but we don't know whose eyes we're looking through. We watch these scenes with a tightness in our throats, waiting for it to start to make sense. We're waiting for the world to be put back together in the right order. Why on earth would the Bible be interested in making us feel that way?

Educators frequently talk about the "disorienting dilemma" as an important pedagogical tool. A particular problem for adult learners is the frameworks we have in place for our experiences of the world; we've lived long enough that we tend to think we understand the world pretty well, or at least we've developed coping strategies that help us get through everyday life by pretending we do. This can make it hard to learn new things. We can learn new facts here and there, but learning something truly new and transformational requires stepping outside of that framework and examining the paradigms within which we live. In order to do that kind of work, we sometimes need to be dis-oriented before we can be re-oriented into a new understanding.

In paying attention to Genesis 32:24–32 as a text of horror, I recognize elements of this disorienting dilemma. It seems plausible that this is what God intended to do to Jacob—shock him out of his complacency, shatter the paradigm through which he understood the world—and it's certainly how I experience the story. I'm not sure I could truly get to the understanding of the life of faith as being a wrestling match through a text that wasn't disorienting, that didn't invoke some experience of horror. (Of course, it's debatable how close we can get to this understanding at all; it might be a truth that we can acknowledge from a distance, but that is fundamentally impossible to understand. At the very least, a text like this helps us get closer.) By relating this horrifying narrative, readers are able to experience at least a taste of the fear and disorientation that Jacob felt on the banks of the Jabbuk river. And, like Jacob, we're able to emerge with a new blessing.

For me, this example helps drive home a truth about horror and religion: horror isn't just about teaching us how to survive—it's also about expanding our understanding of the divine and the world. Horror can be a productive means of instilling a particular type of emotion, and through those emotions get us to a place where we might not be able to get just by thinking about it with our rational minds. Horror makes us feel, sometimes feelings that are visceral and unpleasant. But we shouldn't stop at just feeling. Throughout this book, I'll be looking at how texts engender horror in their readers and asking you to think about what this horror might be saying. As we'll see, this isn't a one-size-fits-all solution to every challenging biblical text. There will be passages that generate uncomfortable emotions, where we're not quite sure what to do with those. But if we can become better readers of horror, we might be one step closer to connecting the emotions we feel while we're reading a text with the truth it's trying to introduce to us.

2 Monster Movies

When I was just learning to read, barely in kindergarten, I remember the public library being a magical place. They had more books than I could count, and I could take any of them home that I wanted. There were piles on piles of picture books, and when I wanted something more grown up, my dad picked up books of Greek mythology and the adventures of Jack the Giant Slayer to read to me before bed. (That detail might provide some insight into why I've grown into an adult with such an odd and unlikely combination of academic pursuits.) I couldn't believe that all of these books were just there, waiting for me to read them.

And during the summer, it always seemed to be a buzz of activity. There were weekly story times, challenges to see if we could read a set amount of books, and times to gather together and play games. But what I remember most were the Wednesday morning movie screenings, when they'd invite the kids back to the big community room and project an old movie on the wall while we all sat on the floor. It was where I was first exposed to *The Wizard of Oz* and *The Sound of Music*—honestly, probably where I first developed my love of movies. But the ones I remember most were the monster movies.

I remember seeing dubbed versions of *Godzilla* and *Destroy All Monsters!*, and the cyclops that my dad had read to me about from the adventures of Odysseus transposed to a different setting in *The Seventh Voyage of Sinbad.* It was where I first saw *King Kong*, and even the James Whale *Frankenstein.* I've often thought back in wonder about how fantastic those summer mornings were—and how they probably couldn't happen today, because someone in the community with too much time on their hands would complain about the appropriateness of showing monster movies to kids. (If your local library still shows movies like this, I'd love to hear about it!) Those movies stuck in my imagination and haven't left, even all these years later.

I'm far from the only kid who grew up fascinated by monsters. And for many, they keep their hold on us long after we've grown into adulthood, long after we've banished any hint of doubt about whether there might be just a small chance that the giant lizards we see on the screen are real. They get into our imaginations, and they won't leave.

Jeffrey Jerome Cohen, in his famous essay "Monster Culture: Seven Theses," took a stab at laying out what fascinates us so much about monsters. He notes that monsters are free of the limits of culture and morality and can do just about whatever they want—a fantasy that's probably occurred to most of us at one time or another. I remember sitting at my desk in a middle school classroom, writing numbers on what seemed at the time like a mind-numbing worksheet, and wondering what it would feel like to stomp through my city's downtown. I didn't really want to destroy anything, not really—I just wanted to be out of this classroom and not having to listen to anyone tell me what to do. Godzilla sure wasn't sitting behind a cramped desk trying to squeeze numbers into a worksheet. Long before I'd read Cohen's essay, I understood that we admire monsters for their freedom.

We're also fascinated by monsters because they show us the parts of ourselves that we have a hard time acknowledging; parts that maybe we wish weren't there, but that in our quieter moments we know are deep inside us. Maybe the selfish parts of ourselves, the greedy parts, or even just the scared and vulnerable parts. We see all those things reflected in the monsters on the screen, and we feel a little better that that part of ourselves has been acknowledged—even if we can't quite put our finger on the connection that we're feeling.

And sometimes, it's just cool to see something depicted that doesn't seem like it belongs in this world, as if suddenly the world has become a little more interesting than it was a few minutes ago because of this new possibility. Monsters stretch our ideas of what's possible, pushing our imaginations a little farther than we're used to having them go.

I think all of these things are true. And that's another aspect of monsters that makes them so compelling—they can be several things, all at the same time. But something else that almost always attaches itself to the monster is a message of some kind. Monsters show us things about ourselves, about the world, and about the society in which we live. Monsters are messages put into chaotic, sometimes terrifying, motion.

We can see this clearly in a movie like the 1953 *Godzilla*, especially in the original Japanese version. Godzilla is a product of nuclear testing, a reminder that we've unleashed something on this world that we don't understand and can't control—a reality that becomes literalized in the form of Godzilla. The fact that this movie came out a scant eight years after the bombings of Hiroshima and Nagasaki gives it an almost haunting quality in the midst of the poorly aged special effects extravaganza.

The Bible uses monsters in much the same way. Sometimes, they come directly from the divine to tell us something; at other times, they're enemies of God, and God does battle with them or otherwise works to contain and control them. But in all cases, they're messages from outside of the everyday, mundane world, messages about who we are as people and where we find ourselves in the universe.

A further observation on monsters was made by film critic Robin Wood in his famous essay "An Introduction to American Horror," written in the mid-1970s when studying horror was just starting to become a thing. He suggests that there's a "basic formula" to the horror movie: "Normalcy is threatened by the monster." It seems like a simple, straightforward definition, right? Things are normal, then the monster arrives on the scene and suddenly everyone's running around in circles to avoid being gobbled up. The heroes come in and defeat the monster, and we can get back to our daily lives. At least until the sequel.

But this simple definition conceals a ticking time bomb at its heart, ready to explode at any moment. What's "normal"? What does this look like, what does it mean, and who gets to define it? And would we really want to go back to it?

This is the kind of work that horror narratives have been using monsters to do for centuries—destabilizing our preconceptions, asking us to reflect on what "normal" means, and insisting we think about whether it's really the kind of life we want to be living, the kind of society we want to have. In the decades since *Night of the Living Dead* burst onto the drive-in screen in 1968, horror movies have become increasingly concerned with this idea, and increasingly subversive in their answers. Sometimes we respond to the monster in terror, but after the monster has been chased off the emotion that lingers is shame due to what the monster has shown us about the world we're living in and the kind of people this world has caused us to become.

Sometimes this is the message that the monster brings us. The monster asks us to look around at the society we live in, at the systems we've created and the structures that sustain us, and ask ourselves if they're really worth fighting for. Or if, sometimes, at least in part, we're secretly rooting for the monster to tear it all down, just so we can see what new world might arise.

Daniel 7 and the Beasts from the Sea

The book of Daniel shows us not one, not two, but four monsters emerging from the ocean. Daniel's an odd book, with two clearly distinct halves. Chapters 1–6 tell of the exploits of Daniel and his companions as they become advisors to a series of foreign kings who take turns ruling over Israel. Daniel uses both his own cleverness and his connection with God to get the best of the king and his advisors, frequently in stories that end with the king recognizing the supremacy of Daniel's God. It's the place where we find the stories about Daniel in the lions' den; and Shadrach, Meshach, and Abednego, dancing in the furnace with the mysterious fourth man. It's also the home of lesser-known but deeply eerie stories, such as when God curses King Nebuchadnezzar with lycanthropy, or when King Darius is warned of the impending collapse of his kingdom by a mysterious hand writing a cryptic message on the wall of the banquet hall. However strange the imagery might be, these are all conventional stories. Each chapter is narrated in a third-person omniscient voice and follows a similar structure of some kind of challenge presented to Daniel and his friends that they overcome through faith. There's a conflict, there's rising tension, and there's a conclusion that wraps everything up (until the next chapter, when the king seems to have forgotten about Daniel and God).

A strong example of this storytelling convention is chapter 6, right before the abrupt shift we're going to talk about next. Chapter 6 tells the story of the lion's den, told by a conventional narrator with Daniel and his friends as the main characters. The chapter ends with this summary statement: "So this Daniel prospered during the reign of Darius and the reign of Cyrus the Persian." This gives a good example of how these stories are told. There's a narrator who calmly walks us through these events, gives some history and context to everything, and tells us how to interpret what we just read.

But with chapter 7, right in the middle of a book, things take a sharp left turn into Oddsville. Instead of a story filled with conflict and resolution, we have a first-person narrative, told from Daniel's point of view. A narrator quickly introduces things, with a statement that sounds like it might be a continuation of chapter 6. The chapter begins, "In the first year of King Belshazzar of Babylon, Daniel had a dream and visions of his head as he lay in bed." But after this, the rest of the book is told from Daniel's perspective, as if Daniel is addressing us directly. And instead of stories, we're presented with a series of terrifying and increasingly bizarre visions. These visions begin with a parade of monsters that would have played well in my hometown library's community room. Biblical scholars note that a major part of this tectonic shift is because we've moved from court narratives to the apocalyptic genre; we'll talk more about this genre near the end of the book.

Even before the monsters show up, we're in a dangerous, mythical world. "I, Daniel, saw in my vision by night the four winds of heaven stirring up the great sea" (7:2), the report of the dream-vision begins. This line recalls Genesis 1, when all of creation was nothing but "formless and void," and a "wind (breath, perhaps?) from God swept over the waters." We're in the time of pre-creation, when all that exists is the tumultuous chaos of the great sea. Many scholars have read in this image a harking back to the creation stories of other cultures of the ancient Near East, where a creator god must do battle with the personified sea in order to create the world. It's a fight between the chaos of the sea and the order that a god wants to shape the world into.

We see some of this struggle in the creation account of Genesis 1. The idea of creation out of nothing—"creation ex nihilo"—is a later idea, one that the actual biblical text doesn't really support. It was clear that "in the beginning" there was already stuff, just stuff that didn't have a form, a shape, or a discernable purpose. In Genesis 1, God's role is less bringing something into existence than it is shaping and organizing. There are some hints of the divine combat that we see in other creation myths; for example, in Genesis 1 God "divides" the waters to bring forth dry land, just as Marduk "divides" the vanquished Tiamat's body to create the earth and the heavens in the Babylonian myth known as the Enuma Elish. But while gods like Marduk had to fight to overcome their opponents, all the God of Genesis 1 has to do is speak.

In Daniel 7, the "great sea" and the "four winds of heaven" that "stir it up" sure seem to pull us back into this mythical world of Genesis 1, a world before creation as we know it, a world where the chaos teems all around us. And it's out of this great sea that the monsters start emerging, one at a time so that we can get a good look at each one of them.

These monsters (at least the first three; we'll get to the fourth later) are hybrid creatures. They have recognizable features of animals that we know, but these features are combined in ways that don't exist in nature, and maybe don't even make sense. This is a standard way that monsters are put together, or at least how they're described. Philosopher Noël Carroll, in his foundational work *The Philosophy of Horror*, identifies two main types of monster: there are fission monsters, those that are created by having their traits spread across multiple identities, like werewolves and doppelgängers; and there are fusion monsters, those that have categories from different beasts jammed together into a single creature. For example, Carroll identifies zombies as fusion creatures because they combine the categories of alive and dead into a single creature.

The monsters in Daniel 7 are bestowed with the most mundane combination of features, but gradually their appearance grows more outlandish. At first, we're introduced to a lion with eagle's wings, something we would probably associate with a griffin today. (The griffin usually has an eagle's head as well as wings, but it's pretty close.) Even closer to the mark would be a sphinx, the kind of lion–eagle hybrid we see depicted in ancient Egyptian art. But if this beast itself wasn't strange enough, we then see its wings being plucked off. The Hebrew and most English translations use the passive voice here because there's no indication of who did the plucking. And then it's lifted off the ground (again, in the passive voice). We're supposed to imagine some unseen force doing this, something that's far stronger than a lion-eagle hybrid. And finally, it is stood up on two legs and given a "human mind." Many scholars have noted the connection with the Babylonian King Nebuchadnezzar, in Daniel 4; in this chapter, God tells the king that "the kingdom has departed" from him, and turns him into a wild beast. The story tells us that Nebuchadnezzar roamed the woods "until his hair grew as long as eagles' feathers and his nails became like birds' claws." Scholar C. L. Seow observes that this first beast of Daniel 7 "reverses the scene of the judgment of King Nebuchadnezzar in 4:10–33."

This connection with Daniel 4 seems to imply, perhaps, that the "human form" this beast assumes might be a royal form. Perhaps Daniel's vision is revealing to us that the kings of this world are actually murderous beasts, placed on two feet and given a human mind? It seems like these few short lines encode a pointed critique of royal power structures—a critique that still resonates today. It would explain a lot of things if our world leaders were monstrous beasts dressed up in suits and ties.

The first beast just stood there as we watched it being transformed into a human. With the second beast, the emphasis shifts to its violent power and insatiable appetite. Daniel tells us that "it looked like a bear"—but notice how much work the phrase "it looked like" is doing here. It's sort of a bear, but not quite. The impression is almost that of a bear that's fallen into the uncanny valley, such that a bear is the closest referent we have, but we know that's not quite right. Furthermore, the only physical description we get beyond this is of its mouth, which has "three tusks" mixed in among its teeth. Once we are introduced to its mouth, it is told (again—passive voice) to "arise, devour many bodies!" While the first beast disguised itself as a human to carry out its malevolence, this monster is just set loose to run amuck.

The closest analog to the third beast is a leopard, something already on the outskirts of our imagination. It is likely that this beast would have been more familiar to Daniel's earliest readers than it is to us, but leopards still aren't known for spending a lot of time around humans. But even here, this beast isn't a leopard—it's just *like* a leopard. This animal that stalks in the shadows and avoids human habitations by sticking to its natural environments of mountains and jungles is the closest we can get to imagining this monster, but it doesn't get us all the way there. There's something extra about this beast, something more intangible and uncanny that makes it impossible to describe. And we see that even this description is only an approximation of the beast's base, for it also has "four wings of a bird on its back and four heads." It's hard to hold a picture in our minds of how the beast can have these characteristics and still be like a leopard—another example of the impossible anatomy that often characterizes monsters. And lastly, we learn that "dominion" has been given to it, similar to the first humans when they stood in the Garden of Eden as God's representative on earth. Like the first creature, this is a beast of royalty.

And when the fourth beast comes onto the stage, we've lost all ability to describe features with any degree of rationality. It's not "like" anything—there's no beast that can serve as a natural analog to get us anywhere near the sheer terror of this monster. All we know is that it has mouths and feet and is devouring and stomping everything it can. And there are horns, even horns with eyes and a mouth. It's a Lovecraftian creation of pure chaos, something that exceeds the boundaries of language to comprehend or even describe.

We could spend lots of time breaking down the individual symbolism of these beasts, as many commentaries have done. For example, most scholars view the ten horns on the fourth beast as representing kings, and the little horn that grows up among them "with a mouth speaking arrogantly" represents the Hellenistic king Antiochus Epiphanes, who famously desecrated the temple in Israel in his efforts to further subjugate the Jewish people in the second century BCE. But this kind of work has been done before, and while it's an extremely valuable historical lens, I'm more interested in what these beasts might have to say to us *as monsters.*

Reading Monsters

As many scholars have noted, these monsters are all linked to royal power. They're stand-ins for the worldly kings and empires that Israel had struggled against for generations. So the obvious point is that the governments of our world are monstrous and are primarily concerned with destruction and devouring. It's a similar point to that which the prophet Samuel makes (in much more prosaic fashion) when the people of Israel ask him to appoint a king over them. He responds with the words that God gave to him:

> These will be the ways of the king who will reign over you: he will take your sons and appoint them to his chariots and to be his horsemen, and to run before his chariots;

> and he will appoint for himself commanders of thousands and commanders of fifties, and some to plow his ground and to reap his harvest, and to make his implements of war and the equipment of his chariots. (1 Samuel 8:11–12)

Samuel's warning goes on for another six verses, outlining all of the things that the king will take, but you get the picture. Kings want to rule; they want to take things for themselves. Daniel's vision reveals to us that what lies underneath those desires for dominion and possession, barely hidden by a surface gloss of righteousness, is destruction. Kings and their governments devour, smash, and destroy, just like these monsters that Daniel describes as emerging from the sea.

Linked to destruction is chaos. These beasts emerge from the sea, the primordial place of the battle between gods and chaos monsters. For God to create the world (or at least create the world as s/he would have it made), God has to defeat the monsters of chaos—Tiamat, Yamm, or whoever else represents the sea and the formless void that the sea points us towards. These worldly kings, by describing them as monstrous bodies emerging from the great sea, become associated with this chaos, with this struggle before creation that must be won before the world can come into being.

It's also important to read on a little further. These monsters are so impressive, so imaginatively evocative, that it's easy to get stuck marveling at them. But that's not what the text does. Daniel 7 moves to a brief scene of God holding court (God is described as the "Ancient of Days") and then passing judgment on all of these beasts. The fourth beast is destroyed in front of Daniel's eyes, "burned with fire" (7:11). The other beasts have "their dominion taken away" (7:12), but are allowed to continue living for a while. Even if they continue destroying and smashing, they don't really control anything anymore—God has taken control. But notice how the passive verbs continue. These things just happen. Rather than a huge confrontation, with flashy pyrotechnics and dramatic punches and counter-punches, these monsters are defeated without so much as a struggle. God is so much more powerful than they are that a fight isn't even needed.

If we pay close attention, I think the author of Daniel 7 tells us exactly how to read these monsters. We first noted the actions they're undertaking—the focus on destruction, the fixation on mouths, and the stamping of feet. But then we noticed how many of these monsters have phrases, or other features, that are associated with royalty. The repeated word *dominion* is a key, as is the connection between the first beast and the story of King Nebuchadnezzar in Daniel 4. And then we looked at how the monsters were responded to, specifically how they were defeated. Here, it was all about the overwhelming power of God.

It's a similar process to what we might undertake when reading any kind of monster story, whether it's a story by Stephen King, a movie we're watching on Netflix, or a tale told around a campfire. Or something in the pages of Scripture, where tradition has built up so much reverence around the stories that we often forget to notice when what we're reading is, in fact, just a monster story. When we look at what monsters do, and what human institutions they're associated with, we can start to unpack what the monster is threatening and maybe even what it's critiquing. Once we notice that the monsters of Daniel 7 are associated with royal power, it's easy to make a conceptual link: in the world of this story, kings are dangerous and destructive, and they don't have the best interest of humanity at heart.

Often, how the monsters are defeated is equally important. Although I wasn't old enough to articulate it at the time, I'm sure my five-year-old brain got the message from watching the nations of the world put aside their cultural differences and come together to fight the invaders from Venus in *Destroy All Monsters!* We can keep fighting each other, the movie tells us, or we can figure out how to work together and tackle the problems we all face—not necessarily literal monsters, but problems like world peace, prosperity for all, and the human impact on the earth's climate. The monster itself is a message, but so is its weakness.

In Daniel 7, we see that these kings of the earth, these monsters with dominion over all they survey, are no match for the power of God. We don't even need a battle royale, or a lengthy description of their defeat—they're just gone. At least, they're gone when it's time. The story also tells us that, even though their dominion was taken away, they continue to live a while longer, presumably to continue smashing and devouring. Even in defeat, these monsters continue to be dangerous. It's a nod to the reality of the world around us, that tyrants continue to rule, but also a reminder that God is supreme over all these earthly powers. And that, when the time comes, the battle we've been waiting for won't really be a battle at all. The outcome's already been decided.

3 What Is a Hermeneutics of Horror?

Now that we've spent some time with monsters, in both contemporary settings and the Bible, it might be helpful to step back for a bit and ask some basic questions about what we're doing when we're reading, watching, or otherwise consuming horror before we dig into some other horrifying texts of the Bible. Let me start by asking a basic question:

What scares you?

It might be vampires or serial killers. Or zombies, or ghosts, or fifty-foot-tall monsters stomping through the city, or ill-defined chaotic shapes full of horns and mouths rising out of the sea, or infectious diseases spreading beyond all hope of control. It might be the world ending, or the world transforming into a nightmarish totalitarian state. Or clowns that hang out in the sewer to lure wayward children. It might be any of these things; whatever it is, chances are good there's a movie about it. Those of us who love horror movies take a special kind of thrill in seeing these personal fears blown up to giant-sized life, projected onto the big screen in a multiplex or our slightly less big screen at home, then put into motion for an hour and a half or so. We love seeing these fears playing out, and we love seeing them overcome—if not by the characters in the film, at least by the credits.

We might be afraid of any of these things, or some other monster or creepy crawly that's not on this list.

But we're probably also afraid of dying. Or of living to see our parents or our kids die. And of failing at our job so that we find ourselves unemployed and at risk of not being able to provide for ourselves and the people we love most. Or even of keeping our job, but just not being very good at it, such that we don't make the kind of difference in the world that we hoped we would when we were younger. Or of finding that the mistakes we've made in the past haven't been forgiven, that someone's still hurting because of them, and that they might catch up to us one day.

We're probably afraid of these things too—and there's a movie made about these fears as well. Surprisingly, it's often the same movie as the earlier list.

There's a movie to talk about almost any particular fear we might have, and there's probably also a Bible story. We saw this in the last chapter about Daniel and his monsters, and we'll see it in the chapters to come about other kinds of biblical horrors. Sometimes, Bible stories want to comfort us, or help us learn about God, or talk about how we can live in community with each other. But sometimes, Bible stories want to scare us—maybe to help us learn about some of these same things in ways that we otherwise couldn't.

Along with what we're scared *of,* movies (and books, and Bible stories) have different *ways* that they scare us. Sometimes, they want to make us jump with a sudden, unexpected lunge from a killer; other times, they want us to simmer in a slow-building dread that lasts throughout the entire film. Sometimes, they want us to look at the way the world really is and react with an existential horror at these truths—and sometimes they just want to gross us out. And Bible stories do all of these things too.

So horror movies work on a number of levels: there's the monster on the top layer and an expression of a deeper anxiety lying underneath. And then there's the matrix of how they proceed to make us afraid of this monster and this anxiety, what tools they use to bring out particular aspects of fear. And some Bible stories—not all of them, but a good number, and certainly more than we're used to admitting in Sunday school—are engineered to affect us in the same kind of way.

Bible stories are not the same things as modern horror movies; movies like slasher films, zombie apocalypses, and ghost stories are all built on contemporary genres with their own sense of structure and form. Bible stories, in many ways, work very differently. But at the same time, there are some compelling points of connection: the monsters are sometimes the same, the underlying anxieties are often the same, and even the ways they try to scare us have more than a little overlap with what we stream late at night.

Remember the questions that we put forth in the introduction: What is this trying to scare you with? And how is it trying to scare you? Based on how horror works as a genre, these are ways that the story or movie tries to convey meaning. Scaring us is a horror narrative's way of showing us the world—maybe as it might be if we're not careful, or maybe as it might really be but we wish it wasn't.

When we read horror this way, with an eye toward what kind of world the story is showing us and how it wants us to receive that world, we're diving into a hermeneutics of horror—one we can take with us when we read the Bible.

It's not a method, like we used to think reading involved. In classic modernist thinking—honestly, thinking that still endures in some pockets of biblical studies and other academic disciplines today—"method" involved developing the right set of interpretive tools. If we had the right tools, we could plug in the text like it was the variable in an equation and then spit out an answer: the correct interpretation. More and more, scholars are realizing that reading doesn't work that way. There's no correct answer, but rather lots of readings that lift up different aspects of the text, respond to different parts of it, and draw from different experiences. This isn't to say that the text can mean anything we want it to; if we read the Ten Commandments and come away thinking it's a story about elephants or roller skating, I think there would be some pushback. The text sets the parameters for how we interpret it. But those parameters are often wider than we've been led to think.

Instead of a method, a set of directions to follow to come up with the right outcome, hermeneutics is a set of questions we can ask, an approach we can take to a text that might help us get more deeply into at least some of the things that it means—and maybe some of the ways it asks us to respond. It's about how we go about the process of interpretation.

Interpreting horror raises a few challenges that are specific to the genre. Like many genres, horror is often a combination of text and subtext—the meaning on the surface and the meaning underneath. So when we ask the question, "What is this narrative trying to make us afraid of?" the surface answer is (usually) easy—there's a monster, or a killer, or a plague, and that's the most obvious cause of fear. But there's usually something else, something the monster represents, or that the monster causes us to reflect on in ways that we might rather not. Figuring out what this "something else" is can be challenging.

The first rule is to pay attention to the text's social location—where it situates itself in culture and what kinds of issues this might be bringing to the foreground. Knowing when a text was written and a little about the historical situation surrounding it opens up all kinds of possibilities for interpretation. In the famous formulation of Jeffrey Jerome Cohen, "The monster's body is a cultural body." It's a body that exists within the matrix of a particular culture, and it needs to be interpreted through the lens of those specific cultural anxieties.

The classic movie *Halloween* provides a great example of what this looks like. It's the movie that introduced us to the masked killer Michael Myers and basically started the slasher cycle of films. (*Friday the 13th* was an imitator that tried to up the gore and cash in on *Halloween*'s success.) As we watch, we're immediately afraid of Michael, his blank expression, and his seemingly unstoppable march through his victims. But pulling back, a few things come to mind. It's set in the suburbs of Illinois, and the characters are all decidedly middle class. Furthermore, the main protagonists are a group of high schoolers, with the "final girl" being a babysitter trying to protect her charge. And for most of the movie, everyone's parents seem to be gone—these kids are alone in the suburbs. As has often been noted, and was lampooned in *Scream*, the young people who survive are the ones who don't transgress with drugs or sexual behavior.

Now we're starting to get somewhere. But what really ties this all together is thinking about the film's release in 1978, just on the cusp of the Reagan revolution. As many scholars have noted, perhaps most famously Robin Wood, this makes it seem plausible to read *Halloween* as an early shot fired in the Reagan revolution, a response to the prevalent feeling in the United States in the late 1970s that society was falling apart, that the nuclear family wasn't holding together anymore, and that the kids were running wild. Michael Myers and his carving knife are the immediate causes of our fear, but the film also speaks to the anxieties of a society that's lacking "proper," patriarchal control.

Is this the right reading of this movie? I'm honestly not sure, if by "right" we mean unassailable and inarguably the meaning that the movie presents, and maybe even that the author intended to convey. But I think it's helpful. It starts with the movie itself and connects it to some of the things that were happening in culture at the time. It takes into account some of the details, such as who Michael chooses to kill and how the film asks us to view them as characters, and incorporates this into a reading that gets at what the movie is asking us to be afraid of underneath the fear of Michael. It makes an attempt to describe what Michael's cultural body is actually made up of. It addresses a lot of the material that the movie gives us and tries to work with it in the service of creating an interpretation. So while I'm not sure it's right, I find it pretty helpful. It explains some of the complicated feelings the movie brings up in me; while I'm afraid of Michael as the killer and feel suspense over what's going to happen to the characters (even though I've seen the movie a dozen times before!), I feel some discord with the value judgments the movie is asking me to make underneath this surface text.

I'm not one who really thinks we should go back to a 1950s model of orderly, well-organized authority structures, like *Halloween* seems to be suggesting. I'd prefer to think less about whether an interpretation is right and more about whether it's helpful—whether it helps me to unpack some of the issues that the movie seems to be trying to address, whether it takes into account the details of the film, and whether it explains the emotions it engenders. That's what makes a reading helpful.

Something that seems worth discussing is the vocabulary of fear: You might notice the words *fear, horror, dread,* and *anxiety* circulating through these discussions. While they clearly come from the same emotional space, there are some important distinctions between these terms. Fear and horror are emotions we experience when faced with a direct threat; fear and horror both have an object. (You might think of the object of fear as being immediately direct, and horror as being slightly removed from this.) While I'm watching *Halloween*, Michael Myers fills me with fear; dread and anxiety, however, are not personified in a particular character or thing. It's more of a vibe: Both are unpleasant emotions that involve the feeling that something isn't quite right, something seems to be a threat, but we're not quite sure what it is—or at least it's not something we can touch, fight, or run away from. So while I experience fear in the character of Michael Myers, the idea of our society's falling into a state of chaos and disorder causes feelings of dread or anxiety. I think of it as a continuum, with the experience of fear involving the most direct object, and anxiety the least. As you can see with the preceding example, identifying the object of fear or horror in a movie is easy; figuring out what's causing dread or anxiety is a little trickier.

But even when we figure out what's causing us to be afraid, we still have some work to do, because that doesn't always tell us where our sense of dread is coming from or why the movie is creating that pit of anxiety in our stomachs. To get at what's driving those feelings, we have to look at the film's cultural context, pay close attention to the characters and their values, and ask how the movie wants us to view them. This work of figuring out how we should evaluate the morals and actions of the characters is important work for any kind of reading, but it's particularly important with horror.

For a brief example of why this matters, I'll turn to another popular slasher franchise—*Friday the 13th*. There's not much of a plot in any of these movies; most of them revolve around teenagers at a summer camp who are stalked by the hockey-mask-wearing Jason Voorhees. (Or, as you know if you've seen the 1980 original or *Scream*, his mother.) They've often been condemned by religious groups and others for their graphic violence, and few offer much in the way of a defense of their artistic merit. (At least, outside of appreciation for Tom Savini's fantastic practical effects.)

But it's not the graphic violence that bothers me, though I'm not a huge fan of it. It's the worldview of the films that makes me want to avoid them.

The main character is clearly Jason; the characters that we're introduced to in the opening scenes of the films are stock characters, without much depth or uniqueness. They're all pretty much generic teenagers with one or two salient characteristics—their primary purpose is to get killed later in the film. And we're clearly not supposed to like these characters. In many horror movies, deaths can be moments of pathos, where we as viewers feel upset by the unjust fate that was visited on a character we'd come to admire. But in the *Friday the 13th* movies, there's no connection between the audience and the characters, and the movie doesn't ask us to feel anything but a rush of adrenaline when they meet their violent end at the edge of Jason's machete. There's nothing likeable about any of them, which leads me to feel the movie is asking us to cheer their deaths, with a basic attitude of misanthropy. It's a nihilistic worldview that doesn't see much that's redeemable in humanity; the film's best answer seems to be to kill 'em all and let Jason sort them out. For me, it makes for a deeply unpleasant viewing experience, but I can only put my finger on that unpleasantness when I start to reflect on how the movie wants me to relate to the characters onscreen.

This is also important in our readings of biblical text. Often, we approach a text with the assumption that it's going to follow what we've come to expect as traditional narrative conventions; there will be a hero, like David or Noah, and he'll act as the moral exemplar to teach us a lesson about how we should behave in the world. But narrative doesn't always work that way—horror in particular. Instead, horror often presents us with characters that are not necessarily likeable as a way to tap into our feelings of anxiety about the state of the world; usually in more sophisticated ways than the dismissive hatred that *Friday the 13th* revolves around. Whole new layers of meaning can open up once we realize that there aren't really any "good guys" in the story, and that what we're left with is a world that's gone awry. If we fail to recognize these biblical texts as being grounded in horror—and don't have some grounding in what it means to interpret horror—we're likely to be left feeling frustrated, confused, and maybe even a little bit betrayed at all of the people who have told us all our lives that the Bible is full of goodness and kindness.

So, as we move forward and study some particular biblical passages and the horror genres that can help to illuminate them, here's a recap of some of the hermeneutical strategies that I hope you'll keep in mind:

1. Ask what the text is trying to scare you with—and *why* that monster is frightening.
2. Ask what you know about the cultural situation of the text, questions like when it was written, what

was happening at that time, and who the original audience for the text was.

3. Ask how this contextual situation can help us build a bridge between the monster that's scaring us and the anxiety that undergirds the horror.
4. Ask how the text is evaluating its characters and their decisions, and whether we're supposed to be supporting them, be appalled by them, or recognize some (perhaps uncomfortable) ambiguity.

And we might add a fifth that's sort of a corollary to number 2, particularly when we're dealing with ancient material like the Bible: pay attention to your own cultural context to see how it overlaps with and diverges from the period when the text was originally created. (If you're interested in learning a little more about the cultural context from which these texts arose, check out the appendix, on historical trauma and the Old Testament.)

It's not an easy process, and it's not automatic! You might notice that these are a series of questions to ask while we're reading, not a list of steps to take. It's not an interpretation machine that just asks us to crank the handle to turn the text into meaning-filled sausage. (You might also note that number three in the list isn't unique to interpreting horror—that's an important step for any type of interpretation.) It's a list of things we can try to focus our attention on, ways we can try to wrestle with texts—especially texts that leave us feeling uneasy or disrupted, texts that leave us with a lump in the pit of our stomach and unsure as to why we're feeling this way when we're reading the Bible. The Bible's a rich enough and deep enough book that it contains all kinds of texts, all kinds of ways to try to reach us as readers, and that includes texts that try to lead us somewhere by horrifying us. To fulfill our part as readers, we'll want to come armed with some strategies to use when we're faced with these texts.

Section 2

Horror of the Self

4 Leviticus and the Flesh

Imagine: The city of Jerusalem occupied by Rome, adults sitting together around the fireplace that keeps their house warm, while the children are going to sleep. One of the adults tells a story like this:

I knew a man once who tried to do good. Whenever he would visit a merchant's tent to buy food for the travels he was always seeming to undertake, he would try to ask for a price that was fair, and not bargain more than he needed to get a price that was good for both people. When he visited churches to worship, he tried to listen to the people and understand what they needed so that he might be able to offer them the most helpful advice. Most of his time was spent raising money for these churches, trying to help them become thriving communities that could share the love of God, and writing letters to them to help them work through the quarrels they had with one another. In everything he did, he tried to be good.

But he also knew there was something inside him, something that was a part of him but that he couldn't control, that had other desires. It was greedy, it tried to convince him to do selfish things, it lashed out in anger and took what it wanted. And this thing was so powerful that he couldn't always say no to it, no matter how hard he tried. Sometimes, it felt as if his limbs were moving on their own, with him wishing they would move in a different way, and the words that came out of his mouth were not his own. This thing that was inside of him grew every day, and clawed and scratched at the insides of this man's body, always trying to get out.

Now, what if I told you that every one of us is like this man, with something that lives inside of our bodies that we don't own and that doesn't listen to what we want—but forces us to do the things that it wants instead?

This is part of Paul's letter to the Romans, reimagined (but only slightly!) as a campfire tale. The apostle writes, "For I know that nothing good dwells within me, that is, in my flesh. I can will what is right, but I cannot do it" (Romans 7:17). There's plenty of horror in the passage as Paul wrote it, a horror that's deeply familiar to all of us. We know what we should do, we know what the right things are, we know how we're supposed to treat other people and live in the world. But we can't always do those things. Sometimes, it seems like we don't have any control over what we do at all, because there's something else inside of us that takes over. The idea that our body might be working against us isn't one that's gone away in the two millennia since Paul first wrote these words.

For many people, the first thing that the idea of horror suggests is blood and gore. That's not entirely accurate—there are plenty of horror narratives that rely on a slow, quiet sense of foreboding, and creep us out with what they make us think about, not what they show us. Movies like *The Blair Witch Project* and *The Sixth Sense* are famous for being able to terrify audiences without showing any blood, and *The Conjuring* movies are rated R largely because they're scary, not because they're chock full of violence.

But it's also not a completely unfair stereotype. For every movie that instills fear in the audience through suggestion, there's another that hits its audience over the head with scenes of awful things happening to vulnerable bodies. While excessive bloodletting isn't a requirement for horror, horror is clearly the genre that's most willing to push the boundaries of good taste—or even to blatantly flaunt its willingness to leap over them. Much of horror is focused on what can happen to bodies. That means how they fall apart, how they can be broken and damaged, and how they can even betray us. Sometimes, it can mean exploring how our bodies aren't always our own, in a way similar to what Paul was expressing in Romans 7.

Part of my attraction to horror—and I'm taking a bit of a risk here, because it will be somewhat embarrassing if I find out I'm alone in this—is that it challenges the limits of what I find acceptable as a viewer and what I want to subject myself to. There's something dangerous about watching horror, because it could go off the rails and push way past that boundary at any time. But dancing along the edge of that boundary is part of the thrill, part of what makes it exciting, part of what keeps me coming back to horror even if the plots themselves don't offer much that's new. Sometimes, it's not even the actual transgressions that stick with me most, but the threat that, at any point, whatever I'm watching or reading could go into a completely unpredictable direction, one that's not hemmed in by standards of acceptability.

Throughout the history of modern horror films, there have been a number of subgenres that tried to push on these boundaries in a variety of ways. Perhaps the first was schlock director Herschell Gordon Lewis, who directed a series of films in the 1960s that took advantage of recent innovations in special effects—and the looser standards of the drive-in movie distribution model—and were little more than excuses to watch bodies get dismembered and have other unpleasantries visited upon them. Pointing out that they have no coherent plot is almost absurd, since it's entirely obvious that the movie is little more than an excuse for gore effects. George Romero's landmark film *Night of the Living Dead*, released in 1968, is often thought of as the first film to incorporate these moments of extreme gore into a cohesive narrative that also paid attention to theme and character development.

The 1970s increasingly became a place for horror filmmakers to experiment with boundaries, particularly as the continued rise of drive-in movie theaters meant that the traditional gatekeepers of movie ratings—the Motion Picture Association of America (MPAA)—didn't have the monopoly that it used to. Increasingly, there were ways to get a movie shown without having to seek the MPAA's seal of approval. *The Texas Chainsaw Massacre* was originally given an X rating, meaning it couldn't be shown at most movie theatres, so director Tobe Hooper cut a couple of minutes from the film and resubmitted it, resulting in a re-rating of an R. Reportedly, a number of theaters around the United States still showed the uncut version under the newly granted R rating.

Starting in 1978, with the release of John Carpenter's *Halloween* and his instantly classic character of Michael Myers, the slasher film became a huge box office draw. And with the introduction of home video, filmmakers found yet another way to reach viewers directly. The censorship battles around the movies in this period are fascinating, particularly the attempt by the British government to declare a handful of movies off-limits to the public. These became known as the "video nasties," but this attempt to ban them didn't seem to stop them from circulating. Rather than ending due to censorship and government bans, slasher films died out for the much more mundane reason of audience fatigue after too many sequels. (*Friday the 13th Part VIII: Jason Takes Manhattan* was a clear hint that this cycle of movies had passed its expiration date.) Still, the slasher only lay dormant for a few years before being resurrected by the post-modern variation *Scream*, and it has continued to find new iterations of its basic formula up to the present.

An extremely intriguing—if deeply unpleasant—detour into violent cinema happened in the mid-2000s with a cycle of films drawing much of their horror from torture. Films like *Saw* and *Hostel* depicted helpless individuals being forced to endure all kinds of awfulness, in some ways matching the endurance test that the audience was expected to undergo. Many scholars have noted that these films rose to prominence in the wake of the Abu Ghraib scandal, in which Americans were forced to confront their complicity with what our country was doing in our name in Iraq.

I remember being enthralled by violence from the time I was first checking books out at the library—those Greek myths weren't just exciting, they were also horrifyingly gory. The descriptions of the cyclops selecting two of Odysseus's men for his nightly dinner, then mashing them against the rocks before devouring them, have stayed with me long into adulthood. There's a primal power to the violence, a complicated dance of repulsion and fascination—one that has been around since long before our contemporary media culture started exploring the precise mixtures of red that would show up best on a particular kind of film stock. Shakespeare dabbled in extreme violence in his play *Titus Andronicus*, and Paris's Grand Guignol theater turned bloodshed into a matinee spectacle in the late nineteenth and early twentieth centuries. And closer to the 1980s, the Italian "giallo" films of the late 1960s and 1970s, by directors such as Mario Bava and Dario Argento, would provide much of the grammar for the 1980s slasher films. (*Friday the 13th Part II* even paid homage to Mario Bava's *Bay of Blood* by re-creating most of the earlier film's death scenes—including the *in flagrante delicto* murder that launched me on my horror and Bible scholarship.) There's nothing new about the violence of the *Friday the 13th* films; however, much-appalled film critics would like us to think there is.

We can also find all kinds of extreme violence in various sections of the Bible, much of which we'll touch on throughout this book. But for this chapter, I'm interested in how the body is depicted not just as vulnerable, but also as disgusting, and even as the site of betrayal. To explore those questions, we'll turn to the subgenre known as body horror—then go back to the letter of Paul and some of the rituals described in Leviticus.

The Body Betrays Us

When we watch a slasher dice up a victim, or read about a monstrous cyclops making paste out of the bodies of sailors, we're confronted with the vulnerability of our bodies. We rely on our bodies to get us through each day, to move us around and perform the daily tasks we need to do to feed ourselves, live in community, and take care of all the responsibilities we have in our lives. Often, horror movies confront us with how easily this system that we rely upon so deeply and intimately can break down.

Horror has always been interested in how the body can transform, especially since early film pioneers started experimenting with special effects. The 1931 version of *Dr. Jekyll and Mr. Hyde* was shocking for its original audience for the way it used double exposure to show the film's protagonist transforming into a hideous monster, seemingly right in front of their eyes. And the transformation scene has been a staple of werewolf movies for decades, perhaps most famously in the still-enthralling scene from the 1981 film *An American Werewolf in London.* All of these stories are about how we can lose control of our bodies—and what happens when something that's been inside us all along suddenly can't be stopped from coming to the surface.

Pushing these ideas even further is the subgenre of body horror. In these films, it's not just that the body is vulnerable. The body can turn on itself, transforming into a site of disgust, brokenness, and disease. In movies like John Carpenter's *The Thing* or David Cronenberg's *The Fly*, our bodies don't belong to us—we're forced to consider how easily they can be taken away and turned against us. It's a question that is also raised by the horror with which the Priestly laws of Leviticus view the body, and that Paul confronts when he confesses how often he feels unable to control himself.

Body horror is often most closely associated with the films of Canadian auteur David Cronenberg, particularly with his movies from the late 1970s to the mid-1980s. In these movies, bodies twist, contort, and grow in all kinds of unexpected and repulsive ways. A man attempting to track down the source of the pirated snuff-video signal his TV is receiving suddenly finds a maw in his stomach (ready to load VHS tapes into) in *Videodrome.* People grow strange orifices in their armpits, from which stingers emerge to draw blood from victims in *Rabid.* And a woman grows an exterior, distended womb that produces monstrous children that seem to respond to her rage in *The Brood.* But perhaps nowhere does Cronenberg's fixation on the mutations of the body reach a higher pitch than in *The Fly.*

Based on the Kurt Neumann–directed 1958 science-fiction movie (featuring burgeoning horror icon Vincent Price), Cronenberg's remake zeroes in on the transformation and dissolution of his researcher's body. The simple story follows a Promethean mad scientist, Seth Brundle, who's experimenting with teleportation. He thinks he's got it figured out, with two pods that can rearrange a person's molecules in one, then put them back together again in the other. But as he tries it on himself, a fly sneaks in, and he finds himself emerging from the destination pod with a few extra molecules.

At first, Brundle just notices some extra athletic ability. But gradually, he starts turning into a man–fly hybrid, which he famously refers to as the "Brundlefly" in his initial excitement at his new post-human state. Pretty soon, it's clear that he hasn't been given a gift. There are moments of terror as he becomes more aggressive and attacks loved ones in his life, but that's not where the real horror lies. The real horror in the movie is in the gradual disintegration of his body, and in his slow, terrible transformation into a stomach-churning hybrid creature. The primary emotion the film arouses is disgust—but also a sense of discomfort in how the movie forces us to reflect on the impermanence, and maybe even hostility, of our own bodies.

These movies of bodily transformation and betrayal have two main points, both of which are explored in the Bible. First, our bodies, at least when viewed from a certain angle, certainly have the capacity to engender disgust. They're leaky, vulnerable, and don't always do a good job of keeping inside all the things that should be on the inside. Body horror takes this baseline level of disgust and cranks it up to eleven. But there's also the idea that we might not be the master of our own bodies in the way we like to think; our bodies can have minds of their own, so to speak.

Paul describes this fear with these words:

> I do not understand my own actions. For I do not do what I want, but I do the very thing I hate. Now if I do what I do not want, I agree that the law is good. But in fact it is no longer I that do it, but sin that dwells within me. For I know that nothing good dwells within me, that is, in my

> flesh. I can will what is right, but I cannot do it. For I do not do the good I want, but the evil I do not want is what I do. Now if I do what I do not want, it is no longer I that do it, but sin that dwells within me. (Romans 7:15–20)

Paul describes an inner conflict, but even more than that a divided self. There's a disconnect between his will—"what I want"—and what he actually does. It's a passage built on a number of dichotomies: there's good and evil, what he wants and what he does not want, his body and what dwells within. He identifies himself with his body: "I know that nothing good dwells within me," he writes, "that is, in my flesh." Some theologians and philosophers have posited that the soul is the true self, and the body is only a container for this self. But Paul seems to reject this idea, by identifying "me" with "my flesh." He is his body, at least here.

However, he complicates this just a few verses later. As he further discusses the war going on inside himself—the law of God at war with the law of sin—he summarizes this struggle: "So then, with my mind I am a slave to the law of God, but with my flesh I am a slave to the law of sin" (7:25). By the end of the passage, he's moved closer to the more familiar idea that his true self resides in his mind, while his body is controlled by other forces.

However, I don't want to move too quickly past his earlier connection between his flesh as "me" and this sin that dwells within his flesh. In that earlier passage, he clearly sees himself as his body, even though his body isn't under his control. In this passage, there's something else living inside him, something he can only describe as "nothing good," as "sin." Twice in this passage he describes "the sin that dwells within me" as what is actually acting, as the force that's driving the bus, so to speak. But he still feels like his authentic self resides in his body, even if that body doesn't do what he wishes it would. He seems to undercut this with the final statement associating his mind with the law of God and his flesh with the law of sin, but I would see this as further evidence of how conflicted the apostle feels, how divided his self truly is. I don't think he's come to a clean, simple answer by the end of this tortured rumination.

Paul could have been referring to *Dr. Jekyll and Mr. Hyde*, or a contemporary werewolf movie, with this description of the conflicted, divided self. It's a vision of the self that contains the monstrous within it, a self that is powerless against these forces that live inside. Like the werewolf is unable to do anything but transform in the light of the full moon, so Paul is helpless to combat the sin that festers inside.

That's one half of this equation, the idea that our bodies are not our own, that our will does not entirely direct our being. But there's also the idea, more at home in body horror like *The Fly*, that our bodies are unstable masses that will eventually disintegrate into something disgusting and inhuman. Here, our bodies' untrustworthiness reveals itself in a different way. It's not what our bodies might lead us to do, but what our bodies literally, physically become. And we see this reflected in the Bible as well.

The book of Leviticus isn't the place where most Bible-readers go for inspiration. It's one of the so-called Priestly texts of the Bible, written in a liturgical style and with a focus on ritual. The Priestly texts often get a bad name. Genesis 1, for example, with its beautiful repetition of the cycle of creation that happens each day, uses this same sense of pattern and order to create a beautiful and poetic vision of the world. But Leviticus can be rough reading. There aren't very many stories, and most of the book is composed of detailed descriptions of how to conduct specific rituals. From the very first lines of the book, we're thrust into this world. God summons Moses and speaks from the tent of meeting—this was where God lived during the time when Israel was wandering in the wilderness, before they'd built the temple, and it seems like Moses has to wait outside. And God launches right into instructions detailed enough that we can only hope Moses was taking really good notes. "Speak to the people of Israel," God tells Moses, "and say to them: When any of you bring an offering of livestock to the LORD, you shall bring your offering from the herd or from the flock. If the offering is a burnt offering from the herd, you shall offer a male without blemish; you shall bring it to the entrance of the tent of meeting, for acceptance in your behalf before the LORD." And we're off on our journey into the ins and outs of proper ritual practice. In my decades of attending Protestant churches, I don't think I've ever heard a sermon preached from Leviticus. And it certainly wasn't in my Sunday school curriculum as a kid.

The first few chapters offer details about what kinds of sacrifices the priest should offer, under what circumstances, and how. If you're willing to dig deep into the text, there's actually some really interesting stuff. The main idea is that people do things every day that pull us away from God, and that we have to find ways to reconcile ourselves with the divine. In order to rebuild that relationship, we have to give up something of ourselves. Since the destruction of the Second Temple in 70 CE, the Jewish faith doesn't practice literal sacrifice of animals; instead, they view these sacrificial instructions as giving us guidance about how we can continue to nurture our relationship with God and with one another. The specific rituals of Leviticus can all be understood as working within this general framework.

For me, where the book gets really interesting (okay, relatively interesting) is when it starts talking about the purity and impurity of individual bodies and how to navigate this complicated system. In the Old Testament, "pure" means something a little different than what it probably means to us today. We think of purity as a moral state: if you're pure, that means you haven't done anything wrong. That's one possible meaning of the idea of purity in the Old Testament, but ideas of right and wrong aren't always in view. There can be moral impurity, when someone has sinned against God or the community, but there can also be ritual impurity, when a person's state of being makes them unwelcome (temporarily) in the presence of God. This isn't a moral judgment; it's just the reality that comes from living in the world. In order to approach the sacred space of the divine, we have to be free of the marks of the profane world in which we live.

The first time this comes into play in Leviticus is in the discussion about childbirth. In chapter 12, we learn that women are "ceremonially unclean" for a period of time. "As at the time of her menstruation," the text says, "she shall be unclean." The Hebrew is "*tam'ah*," which is a different word than is used for a sinful action that makes someone unable to approach God. It doesn't mean the woman has sinned by having a child, simply that she needs to be purified before returning to the presence of God. It still makes me squirm in my chair while reading it, since it seems to express a discomfort with the natural processes of women's bodies. As the text moves along, it becomes clear that these ritual laws are uncomfortable with a whole host of things that can happen to our bodies.

These include all kinds of skin diseases; they often get translated as "leprosy" or "leprous diseases" in biblical texts, but we're not really sure what exactly they were referring to. It seems to cover a whole range of skin conditions, perhaps including more serious ones like leprosy, but probably including minor ones like eczema as well. The passages also have procedures for boils, burns that become infected, and even diseases that cause itchy scalps. In all of these cases, the priest was supposed to examine the individual, administer treatment, and perform rituals to cleanse the individual once the malady had gone away. In those days, priests had a lot more on their plate than just preparing for Sunday morning's sermon.

There are many more circumstances considered, many further concerns about what our body might discharge or become. But I hope that the connection between these texts and the body horror of David Cronenberg and other filmmakers is starting to come into focus: In both Leviticus and these horror movies, the human body is a source of endless problems, of endless potential for disruption and decay. I hate to imagine what one of the priests of Leviticus would have had to do if he had encountered Brundlefly and was tasked with figuring out how to make him ritually clean again.

One of the most vexing problems for both Testaments of the Bible is our bodies. In many passages, the writers almost seem to lament that we have bodies, that we can't be pure creatures of spirit, or beings that don't come into contact with the profane world in any way. But we have bodies that have needs that must be fulfilled in order to function, often needs that are inconvenient—or that even cause disgust. We have to put food into our bodies on a regular basis, and we have to somehow expel that waste that's created from our food. We have processes of emission, which can vary based on our bodies' reproductive organs. And our bodies are vulnerable to disease and innumerable other things that can do them harm in this world, which can cause them to leak, fall apart, or otherwise fail to hold everything together.

While I don't imagine this chapter has convinced you that the book of Leviticus is ideal beach reading, I hope it's unlocked some of the very human concerns that lie at the heart of the text. We're embodied creatures, and that's an inherently uncomfortable thing.

5 Tales of Revenge

If the story of Genesis 34 had been told around a campfire—probably by grownups after the kids had gone to sleep, because it's definitely not appropriate for younger audiences—it might have sounded something like this.

Everyone in the village knew Jacob's daughter; she walked with an easy confidence, spoke quietly but firmly, and had a grace in both her movements and her words that matched her beauty. Her twelve brothers seemed to be always looking out for her, and she was seldom without at least one of them by her side. Her brothers always seemed serious, intent on the chores that needed to be done to run their farm or their household–unless she caught one of their eyes and smiled at them, immediately causing the brother who had been so favored to relax his firm façade and break into a tooth-filled grin in return.

One day, she left the village to visit friends in the next town over. Maybe one could say she should have been more careful, but I think a young woman should be allowed to visit another town without fear. Her brothers must have thought so as well—as far as we know, none of them followed her or tried to convince her to stay home. But on this visit, a young man named Shechem saw her and was instantly captured by her beauty. While she was walking on the roads alone, he fell upon her, and forced himself on her. He felt terribly afterward and tried to soothe her with promises of love; we can only imagine how she responded. As she returned to her village, wondering what she should tell her father and her brothers, Shechem went to his father and asked if his father the prince could arrange a treaty with Jacob's family, and have Dinah delivered to Shechem as his wife.

Shechem and his father came to Jacob's house just as Dinah's brothers were returning from the field. It seemed like the prince did most of the talking—we can only imagine that his son was too ashamed to speak in front of the family of the woman he had just violated. The prince tried to explain that his son had behaved poorly, but he was trying to make things right by offering to marry Dinah, and hoped that her family would understand. Her brothers were outraged, maybe for the violence their sister had suffered, maybe for their own sense of honor and the honor of their family. But they swallowed their anger and realized immediately that if they bided their time they could wreak a terrible revenge upon Shechem and his whole clan.

Instead of responding immediately with the anger they felt, they told Shechem that they would gladly bless his marriage to their sister except for one thing: Shechem's people did not believe in circumcision, as did Jacob's family and all of those who believed in Yahweh as the true God. If Shechem was to marry their sister, he and his entire clan would have to circumcise themselves. It seemed a fair trade to Shechem's people—either that, or Shechem's father told everyone that this was how it was going to be. After they'd undergone this ritual, they'd be able to marry with Jacob's people, claim his livestock as their own, and grow more powerful as a clan. So it seemed worth the short-term pain for these long-term benefits. They all circumcised themselves that night.

Jacob's sons waited a couple of days, just long enough for Shechem's men to let their guard down—but not long enough for them to have recovered. They were still healing up, resting and trying to keep the bleeding stopped, when Jacob's sons rode into the village, swords swinging every which way, and killed all the men before they had the chance to realize what was going on. They took special joy in killing both Shechem and his father. They took Dinah back with them, and took everything that was worth taking from the village before riding back home in triumph. There was hardly a house standing when they were done.

When they got back home, Jacob wasn't pleased—hadn't they found a way out of this mess, a way that was going to allow these two clans to live together? But Jacob's sons held firm—they thought they'd found the perfect vengeance. They hurt Shechem and his clansmen in the same place that Shechem had hurt their sister. Fair's fair.

It's a story of revenge that could come right out of any number of horror movies. And it shows the same kind of queasiness that revenge films frequently show as well, the recognition that this revenge is fair on the one hand—but on the other, maybe it's not the best choice.

The movies closest to this story are the cycle of revenge films from the 1970s, usually thought of as starting with a pre-*Scream* Wes Craven's 1972 debut film, *The Last House on the Left.* It tells the story of two young women, Mari and Paige, on their way to a concert in the city, who end up waylaid and kidnapped by a band of small-time criminals. The two women are taken into the woods, sexually abused, and then murdered. The gang takes Mari's necklace and heads back on the road. Their car breaks down soon afterward, and they stop at a nearby house for help. They are welcomed in, but the owners of the home recognize their daughter's necklace, and realize why their daughter hasn't come home from the concert yet. They take bloody revenge on the perpetrators, one of them in a fashion reminiscent of the fate of Shechem's village. It's not a particularly fun movie and veers wildly between almost documentary realism and some ham-handed slapstick comedy—entirely out of place given the film's subject matter. But it was raw and visceral enough that it became a big hit at the drive-ins and spawned several imitators throughout the 1970s, as well as a handful of remakes in the 2000s.

Another interesting thing about it: It's based on a highbrow, Academy Award–winning arthouse film, an Ingmar Bergman movie from 1960 called *The Virgin Spring.* (Wes Craven was a little cagey about whether he was aware of this connection, but the plot points are similar enough that it's hard to imagine he wasn't.) And this Bergman movie was, in turn, based on an old Swedish legend. But whereas the legend is largely pagan in its context, Bergman's film is explicitly Christian; paying close attention to the way Christianity functions in Bergman's film can help us get closer to how we might be able to read the revenge narratives in the Bible.

The Virgin Spring is set in fourteenth-century Sweden, taking place on the family's farm and the wilderness around it. Patriarch Töre frequently leads his family in prayer. And rather than leaving for a concert in the city, the family's daughter, Karin, is traveling to a local church to deliver devotional candles and is waylaid by bandits. (Karin travels with the family's servant, Ingeri, who witnesses Karin's attack but is not attacked herself.) As in the plot of Craven's film, after attacking and murdering Karin, the bandits stop by her parents' house for shelter and are revealed as murderers when they attempt to sell one of Karin's garments. Töre is enraged but takes time to ritually cleanse himself before committing his acts of revenge. After killing the three bandits, Töre has Ingeri lead him to his daughter's body. Töre offers a prayer and vows to build a church on the spot where his daughter was slain. As he lifts her body up to return her home for burial, a spring emerges from the ground.

Director Ingmar Bergman grew up as the son of a prominent Lutheran pastor and spent much of his filmmaking career working through questions of faith, doubt, and the corruption of the church in films such as *The Seventh Seal*, *Through a Glass Darkly*, and *Fanny and Alexander*. But *The Virgin Spring*, despite its subject matter—or perhaps because of it?—might be his most pious film. Karin is a sincerely devout daughter, though she's also depicted as a bit naïve, and perhaps even cruel to the family's servant. And Töre is the consummate Christian patriarch, leading his family in prayer and trying to keep them on the right path. When the world intrudes on their idyllic existence, in the form of Karin's murder, Töre takes vengeance—but is deeply aware of the cost of this revenge on his soul and almost seems to regard his violent response as a human failing. Both before and after, Töre works to reconcile himself with God despite his actions.

Regardless of the exploitative nature of many of the 1970s revenge films, similar scenes recur throughout the cycle. Perhaps the most notorious rape-revenge film of the decade is *I Spit on Your Grave*, a film famous for its brutality and general nastiness. But even in a film as lurid and mean-spirited as this, a sequence midway through the film includes an extended scene of Jennifer, the film's victimized main character, visiting a church to kneel in prayer before heading out to seek revenge on her attackers. It's not a triumphant prayer, where she's asking God to be on her side and grant her victory. It's a quiet, reflective moment, almost seeming to function as a quiet lament over the actions that she is about to partake in. In the context of the movie as a whole, it doesn't do much to redeem all the viciousness that we've spent the last forty-five minutes being subjected to, or the nastiness that's to come. But it demonstrates an awareness, possibly of *The Virgin Spring*, but also possibly of the relationship between revenge and the divine. Enough terrible things happen in this world that revenge is sometimes felt as a human need. But giving in to this impulse takes us farther away from God, creating a chasm that the individuals in both of these movies feel compelled to try to bridge through prayer.

The Virgin Spring's piety is complicated—Bergman himself was the son of a very strict Lutheran pastor, and throughout his career made films that expressed a deep longing for connection with and understanding of God, along with a recognition of the struggle (often ending in failure for his protagonists) to achieve those connections or understanding. For me, *The Virgin Spring* seems borne of this same kind of struggle; while I don't think it offers an easy answer to the relationship between violence and devotion, it feels sincere in the questions it's asking. *The Last House on the Left*, and even more so *I Spit On Your Grave*, probably aren't quite so noble in their intentions. *Last House* writer–director Wes Craven grew up with a religious background—he graduated from the prominent evangelical institution Wheaton College—but was fairly open about his struggles with faith throughout his career. Even so, *Last House* is primarily concerned with shock value and with pressing the audience's endurance to the breaking point. *I Spit on Your Grave* is even more extreme.

Still, it feels like these two movies find small moments of profundity, in spite of themselves. The short scene where Jennifer is shown in prayer, asking for both healing from the horrible assaults she has just experienced and forgiveness for the violence she is about to inflict on her perpetrators, asks us to reflect on the relationship between violence and the divine.

Genesis 34 is frustratingly obtuse in its own perspective. When the brothers return from avenging their sister, Jacob tells his sons that they have "brought trouble" on him. He's mostly concerned with himself and the future of his family, worrying that the violence his sons have just committed will result in further violence. It's a perfectly rational concern, but it also evades the moral question. Jacob's response is purely pragmatic. And his sons respond with a rhetorical question that goes unanswered, asking their father, "Should our sister be treated like a whore?" The story ends on that uncomfortable question, jumping straight to the next story where God commands Jacob to build an altar at Bethel. (While the stories aren't linked together in any concrete way, I can't help but wonder if this command to build an altar is a response to the violence of the previous chapter—that after Jacob's family committed such atrocities, there must be a way of restoring their relationship with God.) If you're anything like me, you're looking for a clear moral from this story, an easy answer as to what Genesis thinks about what we just read, and how we're supposed to think about it in turn. Did Jacob's brothers do the right thing? Was there something different they could have done instead? If we're going to have to read a story with so many unpleasant things happening, the least the story could do for us is to tell us how to think about it.

A clearer message on vengeance is found in Paul's letter to the Romans: "Vengeance is mine, I will repay, says the Lord" (Romans 12:19; the same phrase is echoed in Hebrews 10:30). Here's a much more straightforward statement about revenge: it doesn't belong to us as humans. We need to be patient and trust that God is going to sort things out. Paul prefaces this famous saying by admonishing the reader to "never avenge yourselves" and to do everything we can to "live peaceably."

Frequently, the Hebrew Bible commandment of "an eye for an eye," from Leviticus 24:20, is thought of as advocating revenge; Christians tend to read this statement as further evidence of the Old Testament's bloodthirstiness, in contrast to the grace of the New Testament. Jesus, of course, references this quote in Matthew's version of the Sermon on the Mount (5:38) and encourages his listeners not to retaliate at all. But if we read Leviticus a little more closely, it's clear that it's giving a different message. It's not one of rage-filled vengeance, but of restraint and even-handedness. And to push the point about not making snap judgments about the two Testaments a little further, we should also note that Paul, when reserving revenge for God, is paraphrasing Deuteronomy 32:25.

Rather than encouraging further violence, many biblical scholars have noted that the passage from Leviticus places limits on retaliatory violence. You can't inflict on someone else a greater harm than what was done to you. In a world where feuds among families could often spiral out of control—as we see in the story of Jacob's family in Genesis 34—the law of Leviticus sought a way to advocate for just punishment, but for no more than that. And for a punishment that addressed actual wrongs but ended the cycle of violence rather than perpetuating it. (This isn't to say that we must take all of these prescriptions of Leviticus as clear instructions for how we follow these cases. As I've argued throughout this book, what's more important is to figure out the basic principles behind the laws and strive for those, rather than to blindly follow the specific instructions. We don't need to continue the practice of capital punishment simply because that's what Leviticus 24 prescribes for the crimes of murder and blasphemy.)

Perhaps just as important, Leviticus frames this law as being about fairness between different communities. "You shall have one law for the alien and for the citizen," the passage continues. It's not fair to have different expectations for the members of our own community than we have for people from without—we have to treat all the people the same. So, when someone commits an act of violence, there's a prescribed penalty. We don't get to decide to treat a case differently just because we like the culprit.

All of this is a circuitous way of saying that the Bible—whether the Old or the New Testament—doesn't really seem to be advocating for revenge as something that humans should aspire to. At the same time, some of the stories in the Old Testament have revenge as a key part of their plot. You might think not only of the story of Jacob and his sons we've been talking about in this chapter, but also of Absalom's murder of his brother as a response to Amnon's rape of their sister (2 Samuel 13). And we might throw Samson's murder of hundreds of Philistines into the mix as well.

This leads to a key point in reading the Bible: Not all the behavior is to be emulated. Sometimes the characters make poor choices, even characters we generally admire. Abraham is a paragon of faith, but his attempts to pass Sarah off as his sister so that the royal powers wouldn't get jealous aren't his proudest moments. He tries that twice—once with the Pharaoh in Genesis 12, and then with King Abimilech in Gerar in Genesis 20. Jacob tries it too in Genesis 26. The best explanation we have for this is that it was a common story at the time, and there were different versions of it floating around. The biblical authors tried to find ways to work it into the stories of Abraham and Jacob. They apparently liked it so much that it shows up in Genesis three times. But the main point is that it's not behavior we're supposed to emulate. There's actually a point where Abraham gets reprimanded and comes across as looking like a pretty foolish and self-absorbed man, willingly putting Sarah in harm's way so that he doesn't risk getting into an awkward situation himself.

Not everyone reads this story and assumes it means that the proper behavior when entering a new town is to pretend your wife is your sister so that powerful men don't get jealous and try to take her by force. It's a story about trickery that doesn't work, and about how Abraham struggles to have enough faith to get through the world even after his direct encounters with God. It's a story about how Abraham is also human and makes some bad choices—just like we all do.

But too often we've been taught to approach the Bible as a set of instructions, as a series of models to live by. These stories are far too complicated for that. And when we encounter stories like the tale of Dinah and her brothers, this view of the Bible doesn't work at all. There's not much in that story to emulate. Instead, we see a messy, violent world where people don't treat each other well. We see people receiving violent treatment and responding with violence in kind. If the biblical writers had wanted to make a story that just told us what to do, presumably they could have done that, but I think they knew that would also be so much less interesting than the morally complicated, sometimes awful tales that the book actually contains.

And this reflection brings us full circle to how revenge movies like *The Virgin Spring*, or even more vicious iterations of the same basic story like *I Spit on Your Grave* or *The Last House on the Left*, can leave us with this same set of complicated, conflicted emotions. Sometimes, these emotions are easier to sort out when they come to us from popular culture as opposed to from the Bible.

When we see Töre responding to the news of his daughter's assault and death with grief, prayer, and violence, we see a deeply human man living with the consequences of the violence humanity has allowed to thrive in this world, and feeling like his only recourse is to participate in that cycle of violence himself. At the same time, he knows it's not right, it's not just, it's not the path that God leads us on. Like Dinah's brothers, he doesn't know how else to respond. But unlike them, he knows that what he's done is unjustifiable, even if it was a response to a prior act that was also unjustifiable. He sees the spring that emerges from the ground where his daughter was murdered as a sign of grace, a sign that perhaps something good can come out of all this violence. But that doesn't mean his vengeful actions represent the way the world is supposed to be.

This conclusion almost seems more in line with the theology of another story from Genesis—that of Joseph and his brothers. It's a long story (it takes up most of Genesis 37–50) and rather amazing for how many twists and turns, characters, and subplots it contains. But the gist of it is that Joseph's brothers sell him into slavery, and through divine protection, some amazing luck, and his own sharp wits, Joseph rises to become a trusted advisor to Pharaoh. Years later, Joseph's brothers present themselves before him, unaware of his identity, to plead for some food to help them get through the famine that has fallen on their land. (Joseph foresaw this famine in a dream and convinced Pharaoh to start stockpiling food.) Joseph applies a few tests to them, which might seem strange to modern sensibilities, but when he has the chance to enact vengeance on them, he veers away instead. He tells them, "Even though you intended to do harm to me, God intended it for good" (Genesis 50:20). The actions of Joseph's brothers were evil, no doubt, but God was able to pull something good out of it. Because Joseph had been sold into servitude and ended up in Pharaoh's house, he was in a position to provide for his family during the devastating famine. It doesn't absolve his brothers, but it at least gives us a wider perspective.

The spring that erupts at the end of *The Virgin Spring* is such a blessing, and Töre immediately recognizes it as such. He vows to compound the grace of this act by building a shrine on the site, transforming the violence that we have seen in the film into something good.

It's harder to see this kind of grace at the end of a movie like *The Last House on the Left*, or the story of Dinah and her brothers. And I don't want to minimize the violence in these stories—or the violence that so many experience in real life—by offering empty platitudes about how everything is a part of God's plan. Part of what these stories attest to is that there is real, true evil in this world, and the world doesn't run according to the law of grace. But they can also point us toward ways that we can be a part of this world, move forward when there are no good options, and continue to look for ways to return to a path that's more loving and forgiving. I truly believe this is the path that God hoped all of us would take, from the time when the first humans were raised up from the dirt of the Garden of Eden.

Section 3

Horror of the World

6 The People of the Land and the Horror of the Folk

Let's kick this chapter off with this story:

Our ancestors faced a long journey, a journey that lasted for generations. When they left Egypt, the people thought they'd be able to make new lives for themselves in the Promised Land; what they didn't realize was that this would be a new life for their children, not for themselves. The journey was so long and so hard, made even tougher by the people's lack of faith, that most of them died along the way. They died of famine, they died of disease, they died of old age. And they died of provoking the wrath of our God through their complaints that they weren't getting enough, that life was better back in Egypt. So, many died.

You know of the exploits of Joshua and his armies, when the people finally got to the Land. The Land was rich and good, as beautiful as our God had promised. But it was inhabited by others, strange people who did not worship the same God we did or believe in living the same way. Even so, God had promised this Land to the people of Israel, so God gave their armies the strength to drive these other people out, to claim the land for their own. Even though they had been a people of little faith, God showed them the power that faith can have. These mighty armies fell before Joshua and his men, and the people were finally able to claim the Land as their own.

You might think the story ends there. But it doesn't. You see, even though the stories say that Joshua wiped out all of the Canaanites, and all of the other strangers who lived in the Land, they did not seem to stay gone. Maybe the Land was so beautiful that they couldn't erase the thought of returning to it, or maybe it's just another example of things coming back to the surface after you push them down. Or maybe it's as simple as what our Book tells us God said to no one in particular: "Because this people have transgressed my covenant that I commanded their ancestors, and have not obeyed my voice, I will no longer drive out before them any of the nations that Joshua left when he died." But throughout the generations after Joshua, whenever the people of Israel would start to forget about God, the Canaanites and the other people of the Land would come back, and we would find ourselves enslaved again. After years of oppression, God would raise up a hero among us to vanquish these foes, and peace would return. But before too long, we would forget the ways of God again, and the old ways would creep back. The people would start worshipping the old gods, worshipping in different ways, letting greed consume them. Instead of following the ways of their ancestors, who had been faithful to YHWH, they followed ways that were older than Abraham, older than the covenant they had made with God.

We try to live in the ways that God has commanded us, to follow the path laid out in front of us by Moses. But those other gods won't stay dead, the ways that we knew before we knew YHWH keep coming back. Our entire tradition has been haunted by these ghosts, ghosts that don't ever seem to stay quiet for long. They keep coming back.

The book of Judges can be a tough book to wade through, though for entirely different reasons than the book of Leviticus. It's not a lengthy list of laws and rituals; it's a group of stories about Israel as a collection of tribes, before King David bound them together into a single nation. This sounds like it should be exciting, right? And there's plenty in the book to get excited about. The story of Samson is probably most well-known, but Gideon's adventures are pretty stirring as well. What makes the book so difficult is the casual brutality that drips off every page, the violence that doesn't seem to follow any moral code or know any boundaries. It's a picture of what life used to be in the bad old days, and what life could return to if the people reject Yahweh—or their king.

As a side note, but an important one, most scholars view this book as being a collection of folk tales and myths, with a tangential relationship to past events, a chronicle a long way from what we would characterize today as history. (Later books, like Kings and Chronicles, are certainly theological interpretations, but are still rooted more closely in the historical records of kings and empires than in the kind of folk tales we see in Judges.) Thus, the violence in these stories didn't necessarily happen just the way it was written down; there was a lot of creative license on the part of the authors. It reassures me to think that all of these tales don't necessarily represent actual, historical human suffering. Still, it disturbs me that the Bible wants us to remember Israel's past this way. We'll circle back around to that issue by the end of the chapter.

The book of Judges occurs at the point in the Old Testament where history is just starting to take shape, where we can begin to see the shadowy outlines of verifiable events quavering beneath the surface of myth. As Judges begins, Moses has led the people out of Egypt and through the wilderness; then, after Moses' death, Joshua has led them on a conquest of the Promised Land to claim it as their own. They've started to settle the land under a loose confederation of tribes, groups that had their own leaders but would band together in times of trouble. We have a hint of this in Judges 5, usually called the "Song of Deborah" and considered to be one of the oldest texts in the Bible. But many of these stories, such as the ones surrounding Gideon and Samson, are clearly legendary in character, shaped to support the ideology of the book's author. For many scholars, that's about making the case that Israel has to be ruled by a king—which will be the main subject of the books immediately following, 1–2 Samuel and 1–2 Kings. Things get pretty dark by the end of Judges, presumably so that readers can easily understand how being ruled by a king is preferable to the violence and chaos that the book presents.

At the same time, the book of Judges isn't just about history—it's about how history can shine a light on the present. The situation that the author of Judges sees is one that's similar to his own time. He sees a people straying from the word of God, who decide they're going to follow their own way and then are surprised when things don't work out for them. When we look at our history, see the mistakes people made, and experience the consequences they suffered, it helps us to analyze the present with a clearer mindset.

But the past is a scary place. L. P. Hartley began his 1953 novel *The Go-Between* with the justifiably famous words: "The past is a foreign country. They do things differently there." While that's true, I'd argue that it doesn't go far enough: the past isn't just foreign and different. Often, it's also terrifying. The past should have enough points of connection to our own times that we can see the differences and still draw a straight line from there to here, but it doesn't always work that way. Sometimes, the past leaves us stuck in the uncanny valley, that place that's similar enough to our own experience to be recognizable, but just different enough to be, somehow, wrong.

Judges leans into this terror in a number of ways. The enemies the Israelites face are often described in clearly non-human terms, such as when the Midianites swarm "as thick as locusts" to "waste the land" as they rampage across it (6:5; they're called locusts again in 7:12). Often, the enemies are portrayed as so powerful that the Israelites have no hope against them—all the people of Israel can do is wait for God to decide that it's time for them to throw off their oppression, a period of waiting that often stretches out for a generation.

But most obvious is the violence that permeates the book, violence that is often graphic, detailed, and intimate, in a way that violence in the Bible often isn't. Early on in the book, the Canaanite general Sisera hides from his army's loss in the tent of a woman named Jael, whom he assumes is an ally and will treat him kindly. Jael gives him a bowl of milk and does everything but sing him a lullaby to get him to sleep; once he's curled up on her floor, she picks up a mallet in one hand and a tent peg in the other and drives it through his skull. Instead of just saying Sisera was killed, or giving a slightly more descriptive word like *stabbed* to indicate a manner of death, we have this elaborate story that details his killer's relationship with him before recounting the blow that ended his life. That's far from the only story that carries this level of detail, this analytical focus on the violence it is describing.

And as this violence crescendos, the book starts to give its readers a repeated refrain: "In this time, there was no king in Israel, and every man did what was right in his own eyes." The cruelty that we're witnessing in this book is a part of this landscape, a result of the lawlessness that happens when people don't have a strong ruler—and don't follow the commands of God.

It can be tough to read these stories and find anything positive to take from them. We know that God is involved because we learn that God sends each subsequent judge who rescues Israel from its oppressors. (Though as the book progresses and the violence increases, God seems to be around less and less.) These stories are another example of stories in the Bible that can be approached as horror, giving us the chance as readers to figure out what they might be trying to communicate. But what kind of horror? They're clearly different from the body horror that we find in Leviticus, or the monster stories of Daniel 7. I think they're closest to one of the more recent arrivals on the horror scene: folk horror.

Folk horror is a relatively new term, seemingly coined in the early 2000s and first coming into widespread usage around 2015. At first, it was most commonly used to refer to a group of British films from the late 1960s and early 1970s—with *The Wicker Man*, *Blood on Satan's Claw*, and *Witchfinder General* considered the founding triumvirate of the genre—along with some of the British television that aired around the same time. (The annual M. R. James adaptations are perhaps the most well-known of these.) And, of course, folk horror also had antecedents, including the eerie stories of Arthur Machen. The term has since been expanded to include films and fiction from many different national traditions, including American examples going as far back as Washington Irving and Nathaniel Hawthorne.

The definition of folk horror can be squishy, even more so than some of the other genres we've looked at in this book. There's often an urban–rural divide, where the modern (but naïve) city-folk run into something more primal and dangerous, either from small-town inhabitants or the land itself. Perhaps most important, the horror is rooted in folk tales, traditions that the urban elite might scoff at but that hold far more truth than they're willing to admit. Folk horror requires a conflict between the present and the past—and the terrifying realization that the past might not be as different from the present as we'd like to think.

If there's one film that most people associate with the folk horror genre, it's the 1973 British film *The Wicker Man.* The movie follows a devoutly Anglican police officer, Sgt. Howie, who travels to Summerisle after receiving a tip about a missing girl. He travels to the remote island and finds a pagan culture strongly at odds with his fundamentalist vision of Christianity. The islanders celebrate procreation, spend their evenings in bawdy revelry, and believe that nature is the true god who must be appeased. As Sgt. Howie becomes more and more horrified at what he considers the immorality of what he finds, it also becomes apparent that there is no missing girl; instead, it has all been an elaborate ruse to lure Howie to the island so that he can become the annual May Day sacrifice at the islanders' harvest festival.

Like the book of Judges, what *The Wicker Man* depicts is a clash of religions. Sgt. Howie is convinced that his strain of Christianity is the only correct way to the truth, a belief that he holds onto until the moment of his death; the film famously ends with him maniacally singing hymns as the Wicker Man he is trapped within becomes consumed by flames. He is unable to recognize the beliefs of the islanders as a tradition in its own right, a tradition that has helped them survive for generations in the inhospitable landscape of Summerisle. The conflict presented in the film is both between the modern and the ancient, and also between two incompatible religious worldviews.

The film seems deeply aware that it can only glorify the religion of Summerisle's inhabitants to a certain degree; we learn from the island's ruler (a delicious cameo by British horror icon Christopher Lee) that the true reason behind the inhabitants' agricultural success has to do with biology more than theology, a truth that has been kept from most of the islanders for generations. And their religion revolves around human sacrifice, with some thinly veiled justifications. Lord Summerisle notes that the sacrifice must be willing, and the islanders accept Howie's willingness to serve based on his entering the Wicker Man of his own accord in his search for the missing girl. This stretches the bounds of consent far beyond credulity.

By the same token, Sgt. Howie's religion isn't treated any more kindly. He's viewed as judgmental, inflexible, and generally unaware of how to process that other people might have valid beliefs that are simply different from his. So while at first glance the film seems to present a contrast between pagan and Christian beliefs, by the end we come to realize that these beliefs are more similar than they might appear. When Sgt. Howie recognizes the fate that has been planned for him, he begins by asserting his faith in resurrection and stoically claiming that nothing the villagers do to him can change that. But soon his reserve breaks down, and he tries to argue his way out of dying through protests that the practice of human sacrifice is monstrous. "You can wrap it up any way you like," he says, to the bemusement of the islanders, "but you are about to commit murder." While Lord Summerisle displays a flash of doubt when Howie suggests that he might be next year's sacrifice if the crops fail again, the villagers are largely unmoved as they proceed to carry Howie to the Wicker Man.

To further cement the connections between these two traditions, as Sgt. Howie's life ends with his singing a hymn to God in protest against his fate, the islanders gather to sing a song from their own tradition, in praise of nature and the cycles of the season. They might be singing from different hymn books, but they're both singing hymns.

The movie challenges its viewers to see the inhabitants of Summerisle as being generally life-affirming, positive-minded people—who just happen to indulge in a little human sacrifice once a year or so. In contrast, Sgt. Howie, serving as representative of the Christian tradition, is a dour, judgmental, self-serious man who doesn't seem to have an ounce of acceptance or grace hiding anywhere in his body. We're used to thinking of horror movies—and most other kinds of movies, for that matter—as binary structures. There are good guys and there are bad guys, and it's easy for us to tell whose side we should be on. But in a movie like *The Wicker Man*, these lines aren't so clear. The sacrifice of Sgt. Howie that ends the film is clearly a monstrous act. But personally, I don't really want to be associated with Sgt. Howie, either. Though we might initially identify with him as the film's protagonist and a representative of a familiar society and its authority structures, by the end we're not sure who we want to identify with, if anyone at all. It's an uncomfortable space to be in, a space that folk horror invites us to enter into over and over.

The book of Judges creates a similar kind of space, particularly as the narratives progress and the society becomes further and further removed from God. For me, the closest analog to the uncomfortable spaces of folk horror is the story of Samson. We might have first learned about him in Sunday school as one of the Bible's superheroes, a sort of prehistoric

Incredible Hulk, but actually reading the biblical account gives me a different impression. And it leaves me in a space where I'm not quite sure who I'm supposed to be rooting for, not quite sure whose side I'm on. There are clearly two different cultures at odds with each other, just like in *The Wicker Man*—the Israelites, as represented by Samson, and the Philistines. And like *The Wicker Man*, we come to the narrative with some assumptions about who we're supposed to be supporting to come out victorious. But these assumptions are undercut throughout the narrative until they're difficult to sustain. Maybe that's part of the point.

Many of the stories of Judges begin in the same way. We learn that "[t]he Israelites (again) did what was evil in the sight of the Lord," and, as a result, YHWH places them under the oppression of a foreign nation. Then there's a brief note about how long Israel served this nation—maybe eight years (King Cushan-rishathaim of Aram-naharaim; 3:8), or eighteen (King Eglon of Moab, 3:14; again under the Ammonites, 10:8), or some other number. There's a turning point in the story when the Israelites "cry out" to God, and God takes notice of them. (It's the same Hebrew word that's used in Exodus, when the Israelites cry out to Egypt under the weight of Pharaoh's oppression.) This crying is what spurs God into action, and God responds by "raising up" a deliverer for them—one of the Judges who will lead them into battle, overthrow their enemies, and then rule over the time of peace and prosperity afterward. At least until the people forget and start doing evil again, and the whole cycle repeats once more.

This pattern starts to feel a little similar to the dynamic in *The Wicker Man*—we know we're supposed to be on the side of Israel, but they keep making the same mistakes over and over again, continually throwing their world into chaos and violence. It starts to feel like they're not much better than their oppressors, and maybe not much different. Not to spoil the ending, but this might be because both of these groups are people and act the way people do.

The dynamic comes to a head with the story of Samson. As children, we learned about how strong and tough Samson was, and how he let his heart get the best of him and trusted Delilah when he shouldn't have, but then pulled himself together, trusted in God, and kicked some Philistine ass. (Okay, I don't remember my Sunday school teacher saying that last line verbatim, but that was the general drift.) We can all have the superpowers of Samson if we just trust in God.

Except, that's not how the story in Judges actually reads. The story takes place near the end of the book, and is one of the two longest stories in Judges—it takes up four chapters in the twenty-one-chapter book. (Gideon's is the only other story that's close to this length.) At this point, we've seen the cycle occur again and again. The people do evil, God turns his back on them for a time, they suffer oppression, and eventually God sends them a deliverer. But by this point in the book, we readers aren't the only ones who are starting to grow weary of the cycle. God is less and less involved, and the stories of deliverance are more rote recitations than dramatic tales of heroism. In his commentary on Judges, biblical scholar Dennis Olson sees the book as "a downward slide and increasingly severe disintegration of Israel's social and religious life." For a biblical scholar, those are pretty harsh words.

The story of Samson starts off just as the others have: "The Israelites again did what was evil in the sight of the LORD, and the LORD gave them into the hand of the Philistines forty years" (13:1). But, if we're still paying attention by this point in the book, we note a couple of things. First, the story has been preceded by a strange list of judges—after Jephthah's death, the narrator moves through three of them in quick succession, barely pausing to list their name, the number of kids they had, how long they judged Israel, and where they were buried. They don't do anything remarkable, nothing is noted about their reign, and there's no indication that they did anything other than serve as placeholders until the next person came along. It seems like history itself is getting bored with this story. When the story of Samson is introduced, we have the same formula that begins a new cycle—Israel doing evil, the nation that oppresses them, and the number of years. This time around, the number is particularly striking: forty is a much lengthier period of time than we've seen before. And rather than announcing immediately that God raises up a leader to redeem Israel, we just move into the story of

Manoah and his wife, soon to be Samson's parents, who are having trouble conceiving. Manoah's most interested in imploring God to help him have a son, not in whether Israel will be freed from oppression. Indeed, once the narrative turns to this long-hoped-for child, the focus is on Samson's actions as an individual—his lust, his anger, his need for revenge—instead of anything he does for Israel. As we'll see, pretty much everything Samson does is for himself.

Samson's birth reads like the kind of "promised child" story we see earlier. It starts with parents who are having difficulty having children; it might make us think back to Abraham and Sarah, or forward to Hannah. An angel (or more precisely in the Hebrew, a "messenger") comes to the parents, or sometimes just the mother, and promises that not only will they have a child, but that this child is going to be really special. In Samson's case, the angel promises that he's going to be a Nazarite, a special kind of priest who would devote themself entirely to God. Furthermore, the messenger promises that this child will "begin to deliver Israel from the hand of the Philistines" (13:5). This sounds great, but one phrase jumps out as being rather odd—why "begin to"? All the other judges were simply raised up "to deliver." Suddenly, we have this qualifier introduced with Samson. It makes it seem like, as opposed to the judges who came before, Samson might not be up to finishing the job.

The chapter ends with Samson growing, being blessed by the Lord, and "the spirit of the Lord" stirring him. (Not stirring "in" him—there's no preposition.) But the first thing Samson does with this blessing and stirring is to demand that his parents "get" him a Philistine woman who caught his eye. Now, the verb get (from the Hebrew *laqah*, which means either to "take" or to "acquire," depending on its form and context) is often used for marriage. It sounds strange to contemporary ears, where marriage isn't really supposed to be about "getting" (or certainly "taking!"), but it's a common turn of phrase in the Hebrew Bible. What's most jarring is that Samson isn't doing this "getting" for himself—he's sitting back and demanding that his parents do it. When they push back—son, isn't there a nice Israelite woman that you might want to marry instead?—Samson doubles down: "Get her for me, because she pleases me" (14:3). You can almost see Samson's pouting lip and crossed arms as he makes this demand. Our initial impression is that it seems like the spirit of the Lord has stirred him to be a petulant brat.

Samson's wedding is marred by a strange dispute over a riddle. It's one that Samson made up based on his encounter with a lion, so it's not particularly fair that he makes it the basis of a bet with some of his new wife's kinsmen. This isn't Delilah yet—Samson gets around a bit in this story. But in a foreshadowing of Delilah, she convinces Samson to give her the answer to the riddle, then shares it with her townsfolk so that they can win the bet. Rather than being a gracious loser, Samson responds by going on a rampage and killing thirty of the townsmen. He's able to do this because the "spirit of the Lord" rushed on him; so far in the story, it seems like this spirit imbues Samson with great power but doesn't necessarily push him in the direction of doing good. There's nothing in any of these actions that are aimed at saving Israel—it's all about Samson's pride and his bitterness over losing the riddle contest.

In the story's next episode, Samson fights the Philistines again, but it's also to settle a personal grievance. Samson's apparently been out carousing for a while but decides it's time to come back and check on his wife, who's been living at her father's house. The father seems surprised to see him, thinking he's abandoned his bride. Instead, he offers Samson his younger daughter. (This is one of those details that makes us realize that the culture of biblical times is far, far removed from our own.) Samson stomps off instead and sets fire to some of the Philistines' fields as an act of vengeance. It starts a feud that ends with Samson's wife and father-in-law being killed by their fellow Philistines, and Samson killing a bunch more out of spite. So far, there's not much deliverance of Israel going on here.

There's an interesting note in the midst of all this. There's some more back and forth between Samson and the Philistines, Samson kills a bunch of people with a jawbone and assorted other incidents. At a breaking point in the action, the narrator briefly interjects to inform us that Samson "judged Israel in the days of the Philistines twenty years." It's easy to gloss over this if we're not paying close attention, because it's so similar to the descriptions of previous judges in the book. But it says something slightly different. Samson is serving as the kind of judge that we've seen earlier, the kind of military and tribal ruler of Israel. But he's not ruling over an Israel that is free from its enemies—he's judging Israel while they're still ruled over by the Philistines. He's more concerned with settling his personal grievances than he is with delivering Israel from anybody.

This finally takes us to Delilah, which is where most of our Sunday school lessons begin. We don't have any indication that they were married, just that Samson fell in love with her (16:4; this is after we read about Samson spending the night with a prostitute in Gaza). We know of Delilah's deception, Samson's capture by the Philistines, and his super-human effort to pull the temple down on his captors. What's often glossed over in Sunday school lessons is the specific request of Samson's prayer. He's held captive, his eyes have been put out, and his head has been shaved, so he's lost his great strength. The prayer Samson offers is a short one: "Lord GOD, remember me and strengthen me only this once, O God, so that with this one act of revenge I may pay back the Philistines for my two eyes" (16:28). It's not about delivering Israel. It's not about giving glory to God, or repenting for his shortcomings in life. It's about revenge. Pure, self-absorbed, rage-fueled revenge.

The story ends with a brief note to remind us again that Samson judged Israel for twenty years. At the end of each of the major judges before Samson—Othniel, Ohud, Deborah, and Gideon—we learn how many years of rest the land received. For Samson, there's nothing but the note that he died and a reference to his having killed a bunch of Philistines. The spirit of God may have given him the strength to raze this temple, but there's no indication that it left him a changed person, or one with any kind of moral compass. Strictly in terms of the behaviors reported by the narrator of Judges, Samson is responsible for an exponentially greater amount of death, destruction, and cruelty than are the Philistines.

As a reader, it leaves me feeling like I feel while watching a piece of folk horror, like *The Wicker Man.* I'm horrified at the thoughtless viciousness of Samson's actions and baffled that we're supposed to look at him as a paragon of virtue, one of God's chosen warriors. Except, maybe we're not supposed to look at him that way. If we take the Samson story in the context of the book of Judges, we can see that we're reaching the end of a long, slow decline. (Things get worse in the story after Samson's, but there's not much further down to go!) The people aren't responding to God, and God seems to have momentarily given up. We know this isn't permanent; the story immediately after Judges (at least in the Hebrew Scriptures) is the grace-filled story of Hannah and the birth of Samuel. But here at the end of Judges, things look pretty bleak.

When viewed this way, Judges has several things to remind its readers about—insights that are just as painfully relevant today as they were in biblical times. First, we learn that the past isn't much better than the present. Rather than being a place of tradition and values, the past that Judges presents is blood-stained and brutal. I almost wonder if Judges was written in response to some contemporary, nostalgia-filled, "Make Israel Great Again" movement. But perhaps even more important, Judges shows us that if we think we're better than some other group of people, we're deluding ourselves. Samson's the nadir of this observation; while he was chosen to lead the people of Israel, he instead wallowed in selfish womanizing and a pointless cycle of revenge.

And here's where I would argue that the horror of the book of Judges truly lies. The violence in itself is often horrific. But beyond that, it's the realization that so much of the violence is caused by the people we view as our faith ancestors, violence that often has no discernible purpose or redeeming quality. We're left with a meditation on history and the past that leaves us feeling appalled by everything we witness, feeling like concepts of good and bad aren't applicable because there's no positive morality on display anywhere. If we consider Judges through the lens of folk horror, one uncomfortable answer presents itself: These feelings of disgust and discomfort might be the point.

7 Demonic Forces at Work

In a country on the other side of the Sea of Galilee, a village was haunted by a demon-possessed man. At first, the villagers just thought he had grown odd; he would stop his work in the fields and stand there yelling at no one in particular, smash plates while his family was trying to eat dinner, and wander around the streets of town in the middle of the night. People started to give him more space, hoping that his madness would run its course in due time, and he would return to being the young man they had all come to know. He took to picking up stones from alongside the road and hitting himself with them, bashing his arms, his chest, even the back of his head until blood trickled out and caked itself dry over his wounds. When his brothers tried to take a stone away from him, he lashed out at them, cursing and swinging his arms wildly. Three of them together managed to hold him long enough to wrap him up in chains so he would not hurt himself further. They chained him to a fencepost outside, hoping to figure out what to do with him in the morning.

But they woke up to find his chains broken, and the man gone. His father found him out in the field, standing over the bloody carcass of a sheep he had killed with his bare hands. His father called out to him, but the young man turned and ran. For months, he lived in the tombs on the outskirts of town, barely glimpsed as a shadow when people walked by. The villagers learned to avoid those spaces, especially alone, especially after dark. If he had killed a sheep with his bare hands, who knew what else he might be capable of?

Whether word spread across the sea or this man just came to visit by chance, one day a healer came to town. This man—this prophet—walked to the tombs and called out to the man. When he saw the prophet, he fell to his knees and begged to be left alone. But the prophet would not leave, for he knew this wasn't just a case of madness—this poor soul was possessed. "What is your name?" the prophet asked the demon. The possessed man looked at him from his knees, his eyes spitting fire and his teeth gnashing wildly, and said, "My name is Legion; for we are many." Like the God of old who refused to give Moses his name, this demon refused to be chained to one identity—he was both one and many, both a single demon and all the demonic forces that have ever been arrayed against God.

On the hillside next to the tomb was a herd of pigs; the demon taunted the prophet, saying, "Send us into the swine!" The prophet did so—as soon as he gave the demon permission to leave, the Legion of spirits left the man and entered into the herd of pigs, and this great herd of pigs stampeded down the hillside and leapt into the sea to drown.

As soon as they had left the man, he sat on the ground, calmly, grinning broadly in happiness at the control he had over his mind once again. But the rest of the village was not so pleased; while the demon-possessed man had terrified them, this stranger with power over demons terrified them even more.

We don't usually think of demons as being helpful presences. They're malignant supernatural forces, beings who cause illnesses, possess people, and tell lies about our mothers. But in the history of religious thought, they've actually proven to be really useful.

Now, maybe demons are real—I'm just a professor, so whether or not that's true is above my pay grade. But whether or not they're real, monotheistic religions need them, or something like them, for the world to make sense.

Judaism emerged from a world that was polytheistic. In the cultures around Israel at the time, each locale had its own god, responsible not only for mundane tasks like making sure the crops grew sufficiently to feed the people, but also for protecting the city from roving bands of potential raiders. If your god was strong enough, your city was safe. If you found yourself being conquered, well, your neighbors' god must have been tougher than yours.

We see hints of this worldview in the Old Testament. The First Commandment begins with an admonition to have no other gods before YHWH—something that wouldn't be necessary to state if YHWH were the only god. But in this early stage of religious development, YHWH was just one of many. But YHWH was the one who was faithful to Israel, so the people should return the favor and be faithful to YHWH as their one and only God.

Gradually, we see this worldview, referred to as henotheism—where there are many gods, but you should only worship one—evolve into monotheism, where there is really, truly, only one God. In the Old Testament, this comes through most clearly in the latter chapters of Isaiah and in some of the psalms. In Isaiah 40:18–19, the author asks, "To whom then will you liken God, or what likeness compare with him? An idol?—A workman casts it, and a goldsmith overlays it with gold, and casts for it silver chains." These other gods aren't gods at all, just statues that people have made. This becomes even more clear in Psalm 115, which contrasts the God in the heavens with "the work of human hands," the idols, which "have mouths but do not speak, eyes but do not see." They're inert pieces of silver and gold, materials that humans have dug from the ground and fashioned into a statue.

When there are lots of gods fighting for supremacy, it's easy to understand why the world is such a chaotic mess. It's a battle of god against god, a worldwide rumble that has one god emerging victorious in a particular skirmish, another god coming out on top next. Since all of these gods are struggling against one another, anytime something bad happens there's a ready-made explanation: some other god won that round.

But if YHWH is the only God, and reigns supreme over all the world from the heavens, this explanation doesn't work anymore. So we're left with a major conundrum: If God is both all good and all powerful, then why is there evil in the world? Why do bad things happen to faithful people?

In theological terms, the problem is known as theodicy, the question of how we can acknowledge evil while still preserving God's character. It's one that theologians have wrestled with since the earliest days of monotheism; the earliest Christian theologians, including Augustine and Irenaeus, wrestled with this problem and came up with a few answers that are still pretty common today. Maybe things that seem like evil acts are actually just God testing us, so they're not really evil at all. Or maybe things seem like they're evil to us, but we aren't able to see God's full plan for our lives, or for the world. Even before these theologians got to work, the Old Testament was trying to think through this problem—the book of Job is a monument to how vexing it is.

In some ways, the easiest solution is to slide polytheism back into the picture through the back door. But instead of having a lot of gods, we have the Devil—and all of the demons in the Devil's employ. Now that God has an adversary, someone whose every waking moment is aimed toward causing God and humans trouble, anything that goes wrong can be chalked up to him. And especially when he's got a whole army of minions working for him, we can start to see how bad things can happen in a world where God is still God.

But there's still this strange gap in the story: If God is still God, why are the demons allowed to cause so much trouble? Why doesn't God just put a stop to it? One answer is, God will, just not yet. It's not an entirely satisfying answer, at least for me.

It's this gap where so many stories about demons live.

For many stories, the answer lies not in God's weakness, but in God's power. Demonic forces may run amuck over the earth for a time and cause all kinds of harm and mayhem. But their powers are limited, and when they're confronted with the true power of God (often as embodied in the church), they'll wither away. It still leaves an uncomfortable tension as to why they were allowed to run amuck at all.

It's also interesting to note the particular kind of mayhem these demons cause in the New Testament stories, a mayhem that carries forward into modern exorcism movies like *The Last Exorcism*, *The Conjuring*, and, most famously, *The Exorcist.* In this story that starts our chapter off, retold from Mark 5, it's not just this man who is affected by his demon-possession—it's the entire community, and most particularly his family. Something similar happens in Matthew 17, when a father begs for Jesus to help his demon-possessed son. Demons always seem to rip apart families.

In *The Exorcist*, the first part of the story is as much about young Regan's increasingly volatile behavior as it is about her terrorized mother's efforts to find out what is wrong with her daughter. And *The Conjuring* is as much about a haunted house and an exorcism as it is about a family struggling with their father's absences due to his job as a long-haul trucker. When the Warrens come to help, before they start exorcising, Ed takes some time to work on the family car and make a pancake breakfast. In order for the demonic force to truly be driven away, they have to learn how to be a family together.

In many ways, exorcism films are the most conservative of horror genres. They not only posit that the power of the church is all that can keep evil at bay, but that evil is able to shoehorn its way into our lives through the cracks in our family relationships. We don't have enough of a backstory for the demoniac in Mark 5, or the other demon-possessed people that Jesus encounters, to know if this pattern holds true in the New Testament as well; but the fact that families are so prevalent in these exorcism stories seems to imply that there's a strong connection. The exorcism of Luke 9 even ends with Jesus giving the boy "back to his father" after the demon has left (Luke 9:42).

But something fascinating happens between Jesus driving Legion into the herd of swine and Regan's head spinning around; the gender of the possessed person undergoes a switch. In the New Testament, the most common people to become possessed are young men—with the notable exception of Mary Magdalene and her seven demons. But starting with *The Exorcist* in the early 1970s, young women are more frequently the target of demonic forces, waiting for a male exorcist to come and rescue them. It might be an outgrowth of the inherently patriarchal nature of these narratives—the female in distress who has no choice but to wait until an authoritative male arrives to help.

That's probably true, at least in part. There's also another reading that runs alongside this one, one first articulated by scholar Carol Clover in the early 1990s. In her famous article "Her Body, Himself," she noted how frequently exorcism narratives center on a possessed young girl—but she's not really the point of the story. The real struggle is the faith crisis being undergone by the exorcist, with the tormented young woman as stage dressing for his angst-filled internal debates over his doubts and mistakes he's made in his life. In *The Exorcist*, we first meet Father Karras as a priest with a background in psychology, struggling to keep his feet in both worlds. And he has some serious issues of guilt over his relationship with his deceased mother, which the possessed Regan famously exploits with some choice images of what Father Karras's mother might be up to in the afterlife. Regan is there for the bodily-fluid pyrotechnics, sure. But she's really only a prop; the actual story is about the growth and struggle of Father Karras. *The Exorcist* is the most blatant of these, but the pattern persists through exorcism movies that made their way to streaming services and multiplexes in the 2020s.

One movie that intentionally breaks the pattern is the 2024 Russell Crowe vehicle *The Exorcism. Scream* screenwriter Kevin Williamson was one of the film's producers, so viewers might expect some postmodern winks, and they get more than a few. The film's main protagonist is Anthony, a struggling actor who seemingly self-immolated his career in a downward spiral of alcohol and drugs and is trying to make a comeback as the world-weary priest in an exorcism film. His estranged daughter was kicked out of boarding school, and as punishment is commanded to hang around the film set for some forced bonding time with her father. But the film takes the idea of a "cursed movie" literally; during the filming, Anthony becomes increasingly unhinged in ways that lead us to wonder whether he's relapsing or if the film-within-a-film's subject matter might be attracting evil forces.

The film is acutely aware of the history of exorcism films, and it seems to assume its audience will be too. The first line we hear is Anthony's predecessor (an actor who didn't make it to filming in his role as priest) reading his lines as he walks through the film set: "I'm losing my faith," he begins. The character might as well be Father Karras. And it's a similar story of an elderly, doubt-ridden priest having to put his life and faith on the line for a possessed young woman. But in the world outside of this film, it's Anthony whose body is the host for a demon, and his daughter who has to overcome her own doubts to free him.

After touching on these issues of faith, family, and gender, it's worth taking stock and returning to the guiding questions of this book: What are exorcism narratives asking us to be afraid of? The discussion up to this point has given us a couple of clues.

First, these stories ask us to examine how fragile our families can be. If you've had the experience of having someone in your family struggling with mental illness, or perhaps a parent or other relative struggling with cognitive decline, you know how devastating these challenges can be for everyone involved. It's not just the person directly afflicted who is impacted, but also everyone around who gets dragged into the vortex. While we understand that things like clinical depression, schizophrenia, or borderline personality disorder don't come from demonic forces, the impact on families is pretty similar to what the Gospels describe. They leave family units in tatters, torn apart and at the whims of forces completely outside of their control.

And these stories force us to ask where God is in all of this demonic activity, and why God doesn't intervene to put things right again. This might be an implicit thread that runs through the stories, like Mark's tale of the demoniac who lives on the outskirts of town, or it may be something that's right on the surface, as when Father Karras struggles with what faith in God looks like in a world where evil can do so much damage.

Many of these films try to give an answer to this question, at least in part. I discussed *The Last Exorcism* at length in my previous book, *Lurking Under the Surface*, so I won't give a full reading of the film here; suffice it to say that the film follows the exploits of a con-man pastor who's made a career off performing phony exorcisms. But when he runs into a true case of demonic possession, he finds that his party tricks are a poor substitute for deep faith, and that he's spent his life treating evil in the most deeply unserious manner imaginable. The film presents two major ideas regarding questions of faith and evil. The first is to take evil seriously; the second is to recognize the importance of a deep and abiding faith, as opposed to one that just goes through the motions.

The *Conjuring* films have some important reflections on this question as well. Ed and Lorraine Warren are paranormal investigators called to help out the Perron family, as the family has come to believe that their farmhouse is haunted. Ed and Lorraine find that the haunting is real, but that the spirits aren't simple ghosts, but rather demonic forces. (They explain that ghosts are the spirits of people who were once alive; demons don't have that attachment to humanity.) Ed and Lorraine try to make contact with the Vatican to receive permission to perform an exorcism, but they can't work their way through the proper channels in time and make the decision to perform an ad-hoc exorcism on their own authority. It's successful, but after they return home they're greeted with a message from the church: their request to perform an exorcism has been approved. The church is right in its identification of the evil that Ed and Lorraine have identified, but too hierarchical and bureaucratic to be of any help. It's an interesting comparison with *The Exorcist*; when *The Exorcist* was released in the early 1970s, church influence in the United States was still at a high point, though starting to decline. But by the time *The Conjuring* was released in 2013, the church had been through decades of abuse scandals and political fights and had seen its influence over society drastically reduced. *The Conjuring* seems to reflect this climate—the church might be right, but it's become irrelevant. The most powerful force is the individual believer. (This is one of a number of things about this movie that I find troubling!)

In essence, the exorcism subgenre serves to reassure us that the world is an okay place. There are disruptions, including terrifying ones caused by demonic forces that seek to do us harm. But in the end, faith can win out. Even an exorcist movie that has a bleak and dour ending, like *The Last Exorcism*, has this reassuring message. In the world of this film, inadequate faith is no match for true evil. The corollary is that a strong faith is. It's another one of these horror genres that, in many ways, serves to support the status quo—a vision like the Universal monster pictures of the 1930s or the science fiction horror movies of the 1950s.

In this worldview, the monster comes to disrupt, whether it's a giant bug or a demon. But society will prove itself strong enough to overcome this challenge and get life back to normal for all the good citizens of the world. The role of normalizing force might be the military, or science, or the church, but these institutions all serve the same function. It's a picture that's only slightly complicated when we move into more contemporary exorcism movies, where the institutional church is no longer effective. It's still the basic, traditional forces of faith that can protect us from evil. It's just that these forces are now wielded by the individual, not the institution. Society is still defended, and we can go back to our everyday lives after this brief monstrous interruption.

It's really the same function that the Gospel narratives about demon-possessed people serve. In the story Mark tells about the demoniac, an entire village has been disrupted by the demon-possessed man. When Jesus arrives, the community is in tatters, seemingly at their wits' end in dealing with this disruptive force in their midst. But Jesus sends the Legion marching out into the ocean and puts the community back together again (even if they're too overwhelmed by what just happened to appreciate it).

For me, exorcism movies are another example of how we can find hope in surprising places. This becomes especially apparent when we read them alongside the exorcism stories about Jesus, which foreground the power of God to banish evil. It's a hope that can sometimes get lost in all the pea-soup spewing, finger-bone snapping mayhem that the demonic forces spend most of their screen time creating in contemporary movies—but one that's clearly there.

And while there's little danger of losing the focus on God's power when we read these stories in the Bible, hopefully thinking of them in connection with more contemporary stories serves the function of opening them up a little, expanding what they can do for us. They're about God's power over evil, of course, but also about how evil disrupts our families and our communities, and how important the work of healing these breaches can be. When they focus our attention on these things, maybe there's something helpful about demons after all.

8 The Books of Kings, but Really the Books of War and Destruction

We all know that war can lead people to do terrible things. But one of the most terrible stories I've ever heard isn't about what being a solider in a war leads people to do, but what can happen to people who are caught in the middle of a war, people like you and me just trying to live our lives.

It happened to our ancestors a few centuries ago. Aram had laid siege to much of our country. Rather than attacking and risk losing their soldiers, they were just going to camp outside Israel's walls and let hunger and thirst do their work for them. There was no food for anyone to eat, or fuel for anyone's fire—even donkeys' heads were fetching outrageous prices in the marketplace, and people were so desperate for something to burn that even dove shit had become something to buy and sell. It was a bad time to live through.

Two women hadn't eaten for days and were starting to waste away. Their husbands no longer had the strength to go out and work, their children spent all day crying. So the two of them thought about what they might be able to do. The only plan they came up with was horrible, one so terrifying that no one would ever think of it except at the most desperate and evil of times. But each of them had a young child; they thought if they killed their children and divided the meat up among the rest of their family, they might be able to stave off starvation for a few more days. So, they agreed that they'd kill one of their children and eat together, then a few days later kill a child from the other family and share him as well.

They drew lots to see whose child would be killed first. The woman who drew the short stick didn't have enough strength left to wail but collapsed onto the ground in sobs as her neighbor tried to console her. But they agreed that they would kill the first child together, late at night, while their families were sleeping. They met as the moon was high in the sky, carrying a newly sharpened hunting knife. They crept into the family's sleeping room silently, and the child's mother gently put her hand on his forehead, then drew the knife across his throat as sharp and quick as she could. The other woman covered his mouth as the life drained out of him. They prepared his flesh the next day like they would the flesh of any farm animal, and ate together in silence, their bodies grateful for the nourishment, their spirits sick almost to death.

Days later, the time came for the other half of this terrible bargain to be fulfilled. But when the woman came to her neighbor to help with this second killing, the child's mother lifted her palms up to the sky. "My boy has disappeared," she said, "I do not know where he has gone." Of course this was a lie. Of course she had hidden him. The mother of the dead child slapped her neighbor hard across the face and demanded that she reveal where she had hidden her son, but the woman said nothing. The grieving mother knew in the depths of her heart that she had killed and eaten her own flesh and blood for just a few days' nourishment and had gotten nothing in return.

This is an imaginative expansion on a brief note from 2 Kings 6:26–31. It's such a short detail, embedded within a longer story about Aram's siege, that it's easy to gloss right over as you're reading, but the outline of the events is horrifying. It's a powerful example of how horror can sometimes give us insights into war that other genres aren't equipped to provide.

The Hebrew Bible covers a long period of Israel's history. For most scholars, the actual history starts around 1000 BCE, with the reign of David; the events before that are a kind of collective memory, but probably less reliable than we usually think of history as being. And it ends with the events of the Seleucid empire, in the second century BCE. So, we've got a span of almost a thousand years, give or take. For most of that time, Israel was in the crosshairs of one empire or another. If they weren't actively engaged in a war, the threat of one was on the horizon.

But even though the texts were written about times of war and likely written to an audience that was experiencing the effects of wars directly through displacement and the loss of their homes and communities if not actual ongoing violence, it's surprising how little the Old Testament directly discusses the negative effects of war on the population. We learn a lot about the battles of Joshua, and the campaigns that the judges waged to drive away other tribes. So there's clearly plenty of war; at the same time, stories like this one from 2 Kings, where we learn about the experience of people suffering in Jerusalem during a protracted siege, are few and far between.

Frequently, the stories of war are stories about triumph, glory, and faith in God. We have a few hints of the costs of war on the soldiers and their families—a key part of King David's plot against Uriah, for example, was David's attempt to lure Uriah back to spend a night with his wife, Bathsheba, even though sexual contact was not permitted for soldiers going off to battle (2 Samuel 11). Mostly, we don't have much of a sense of how war can extend its reach far beyond the battlefield. These are realities about which the text, by and large, remains silent.

Many scholars have noted this about the prophets, in particular. Ezekiel, for example, talks about the impending Babylonian invasion, warning the people that they are about to experience the consequences of having turned away from God. And the back half of Ezekiel's book is all about the restoration of the temple after its destruction. But the actual invasion of Jerusalem itself sits in the middle of the book as a big lacuna, something that is assumed but not talked about. In many ways, it's a classic response to trauma. The prophets report the experiences before and after, but the event itself is left unspoken.

In the same way, there are very few horror movies that engage with the experience of war directly. Many war films contain scenes that are clearly horrific—the scene of soldiers storming the beach at Normandy in *Saving Private Ryan* is one of many whose graphic violence sears itself into viewers' memories. But, with just a handful of exceptions, when horror movies want to talk about war, they decide to come at it from a sideways angle. It might be a veteran suffering from PTSD and going down a fever-nightmare rabbit hole, like *Jacob's Ladder*, or a film where everything is covered in a haze or hallucinations and refracted memories, like *A Field in England.* Broaching the subject directly risks being too overwhelming, too *real* to do any kind of the work of processing the horrors that horror narratives usually aim for. So instead, horror movies find different ways to help us think about the horrors—some of them productive, some of them maybe less so.

Falling into what seems to me to be the category of less-than-healthy ways of processing the horrors of war is the cycle of films from the early 2000s where the primary horror centered around torture. In movies such as *Hostel* and *Saw* (okay, I really like the first *Saw*, but the sequels turn into nothing but pure torture machines, with storylines that hardly seem to matter), the primary tension comes from watching a helpless victim being subjected to all sorts of awful violence on their body. It's less about escaping the killer and more about enduring punishment—and it becomes a sort of endurance test for the audience as well. But these films became hugely popular right at the time that the photos from Abu Ghraib were coming out, right as major media outlets were reporting on the United States' "enhanced interrogation" techniques and our processes of "extraordinary rendition" through which we'd hand over suspected terrorists to other countries to do our dirty work for us. We were being faced with what our country was doing in our name, faced with the torture that our tax dollars were supporting and that we were all, in some way, morally culpable for. Being confronted with versions of this reality on the screen allowed us to undergo some kind of masochistic process of absolving ourselves, making ourselves once again innocent through the cinematic punishment we were inflicting upon ourselves.

I try to avoid being overly judgmental about others' tastes in movies. But I have a hard time finding much that's redeeming in most of these films, and I think they wallow in a deeply shameful piece of American history without doing much to comment on it. Instead of helping us come to terms or reckon with these horrors, this crop of torture-laden cinema serves as a kind of exorcism, wiping away the sins of the nation.

But there are many ways by which horror movies can do a much more helpful job of helping nations process their war-inflicted trauma and grief.

Historian W. Scott Poole argues that the history of horror movies is entirely wrapped up in the history of war, and particularly the effect these wars have on the population at large. Poole notes the cycle of silent films in the 1920s, frequently starring Lon Chaney, that featured a main character who was heavily disfigured and often felt like an outcast because of this. Perhaps most famous are Chaney's portrayals of *The Hunchback of Notre Dame* (1923) and *The Phantom of the Opera* (1925), but he starred in a number of other features with similar themes. Part of this has to do with Chaney's gifts for make-up and physical acting; his 1920 film *The Penalty* had him starring as a legless man, an effect achieved through a complicated apparatus that involved Chaney's knees resting in buckets on the ground, while his legs were bent backward and strapped together by a leather harness. But as Poole convincingly argues, there's a plausible reason why these films struck such a chord with audiences: This was the time when soldiers were coming home after the Great War, surviving wounds that would have been fatal in prior wars. But with advances in both surgical techniques and antibiotics, soldiers who would have died of infection or other causes previously were able to survive, albeit with the loss of legs, arms, or other limbs. Chaney's portrayals of these distorted bodies, combined with damaged psyches, seemed to offer audiences a way to come to grips with what they were witnessing in the aftermath of the war.

A similar movement happened in Germany, a country even more torn apart by the war than was the United States. This same time period saw the introduction of German expressionism in films such as *The Cabinet of Dr. Caligari* (1920) and *Nosferatu* (1922). These films featured sets composed of sharp, unnatural angles and stark lighting, creating worlds that looked like a nightmare version of a Dr. Seuss book. These are the films that really laid the groundwork for the modern horror movie; even if you haven't seen them, you're sure to recognize some of the more famous images, such as the shadow of Count Orlok's unnaturally long fingers stretching across the walls, or the mad Cesare stumbling through a demented funhouse of stairs. For Poole, these films are attempts to place soldiers' experience of shellshock in narrative form, and perhaps to narrate the trauma of the entire German nation.

Interestingly, these films are not *about* war, not directly. *Nosferatu* is a thinly veiled retelling of Bram Stoker's *Dracula*, so thinly veiled that Stoker's widow almost succeeded in having the film destroyed for copyright violation. *The Cabinet of Dr. Caligari* is about a traveling showman whose act contains a dangerous secret. Similarly, Lon Chaney's films follow characters with broken bodies trying to make their way in society; there's little of the war encroaching on this world.

But in other ways, these films are all about war; not in terms of their plots, but in terms of how they connect with the audience's experiences. When veterans saw Lon Chaney's characters on screen, struggling to live in a world with a body that had been traumatized, they might have recognized themselves or their fellow soldiers. And when civilians saw these films, they too likely had that same feeling of recognition—if it wasn't their own family members who had returned broken from the war, they certainly knew people who had. And when they saw this dramatized on the screen, maybe they were able to feel a little less alone.

Putting reality directly on the screen can be risky; sometimes, if we're confronted with our traumatic experiences too directly, we have the tendency to resist, to either stop watching or just shut down and stop processing. If it feels too real, we tune it out.

But when a narrative gives voice to these experiences from a sideways angle, we're able to listen more closely, to reflect, and to work through the difficult experiences we've lived through—even if we're not aware that's what we're doing. So, while a movie might not be able to talk about shellshock directly (at least in 1920), having the twisted, discordant world of *The Cabinet of Dr. Caligari* presented on the screen as a sort of next-door neighbor to that experience can help us in ways that a more direct encounter might not.

When the Old Testament deals with the horrors of war, it often works in a similar manner. The passage from 2 Kings that begins this chapter is, in some ways, shocking for how direct it is—it's a brief narrative, set within a time of war, that clearly talks about the horrifying experiences the people of Israel lived through. But in other ways, it's got a few distancing effects that allowed the earliest readers to view it as a few degrees removed from their experience, making it a horror that was still, in some ways, safe to encounter.

First, we note that it's a story about the siege of Aram during the reign of King Jehoram, taking place probably around 850 BC. So, we're several centuries removed from when the book of Kings was composed; this event is already in the distant past. It might have resonated with the exilic audience of the book but also allowed them to keep themselves at arm's length from the events. Next, it's situated in the Northern Kingdom of Israel—this is a part of the Bible's history that routinely drives my students crazy. Let's see why this matters.

After Solomon's reign, the kingdom was handed over to his son Rehoboam. Rehoboam didn't have the wisdom of his father but thought that if he ruled with an iron fist the people would fall in line. Instead, people rebelled against his orders, and the kingdom of Israel split into two parts: the Northern Kingdom, known as Israel, and the Southern Kingdom, known as Judah. Jerusalem was the capital of this Southern Kingdom. The Northern Kingdom was taken over by Assyria in 722 BC, so most of the story of the Old Testament is centered around the Southern Kingdom of Judah. Sometimes, Israel gets used as a term for the nation as a whole; at other times, Israel means specifically the Northern Kingdom. In this story, the reference is clearly to the Northern Kingdom, not to the nation as a whole.

Why this matters is that the audience for the Old Testament was, primarily, the people of the Southern Kingdom. So not only does this story take place in the past, but it's also not about them. It's about the suffering of their neighbors, not their own people. The story has at least two points where it's removed from the direct experience of its earliest readers, both through time and through nationality.

Even more than these factors is how the story is presented. It's part of a series of narratives concerning Elisha the prophet, narratives that frequently include miracles and other mystical occurrences. These stories fit rather strangely within the larger historical narratives of the book of Kings. And in the midst of these stories about Elisha the prophet, there's this story about the king of Israel (he's not named in this story, but context seems to imply that he's King Jehoram) walking along the walls of the city—probably Samaria, the capital of the Northern Kingdom—during a siege. He hears one of his subjects tell this story and is understandably distressed. So, he summons Elisha to put a good word in for the city to God, and the Aramean army departs. If it was this easy to break the siege, one wonders why the king or Elisha didn't do anything about it before.

But in the midst of all this, an unnamed woman gives this report of a truly horrifying tale involving infanticide (though we don't know exactly how old the kids were), cannibalism, betrayal, all done out of utter desperation. We don't witness this event happening directly; we only hear about it from an unnamed woman, who disappears from the story as quickly as she enters. And we hear about it from the King's perspective—and he's not even the main character of this portion of the book of Kings. So, we're three degrees removed from our story's protagonist, learning about this terrible story from a character with whom we have no prior relationship, and hearing it so quickly that it almost passes right over us.

I would suggest that all of these are distancing techniques, ways to help soften the impact of such a story. Rather than give the blow-by-blow details of what happened, how all of the people involved came to the decision, details of how the son was killed, and everything else, we just receive a quick summary account. The idea of how horrible war can be is introduced but moved over quickly—though for many readers, it's a detail that keeps coming back after we've finished reading.

It bears some resemblance to another deeply troubling passage in the Old Testament. For me, it calls to mind Psalm 137, another passage that ends with shocking violence against children. It begins as a mournful, plaintive plea about life in exile: "By the rivers of Babylon, there we sat down and there we wept as we remembered Zion." You might hear the reggae group The Melodians singing their well-known rendition in your mind as you read. But the psalm takes a sharp left turn at the end into a verse that Old Testament scholar Walter Brueggemann has called "unrestrained, reckless, and shameless." The psalm ends with this declaration:

> 8 O daughter Babylon, you devastator!
> Happy shall they be who pay you back
> what you have done to us!
> 9 Happy shall they be who take your little ones
> and dash them against the rock!

It's jarring, discordant, and deeply upsetting. To have "happiness" connected with such a barbaric image seems particularly obscene.

But like 2 Kings 6, this is a story of war and what it does to people. After the people have experienced such suffering—being violently displaced, having their temple and homes destroyed, and being mistreated in exile—the only power they have left comes from bloodthirsty fantasies of revenge. More than one scholar has suggested that this particular image might be rooted in experiences the people of Israel suffered at the hands of the invading Babylonian army themselves. As they were forced to witness their own children being murdered, so they wish for their oppressors.

In both of these stories, we notice the effects of war falling on innocent children. In the story from the unnamed woman in Kings, this is her child who was killed to provide food for starving families; and in Psalm 137, it's the unnamed psalmist who wishes brutal death upon the children of his enemies, likely in response to atrocities that he either witnessed himself or heard of from other victims. Both of these are brief images of horror that function on two levels: the senseless death war inflicts upon children—and the monsters that war can turn innocent bystanders into. In both cases, these stories are too horrible for the text to dwell on at length. The story from 2 Kings moves immediately onto Elisha calling on God to redeem the city from the Aramean invaders, and the violence of Psalm 137 is directly followed by the joyous Psalm 138, with David giving his praise to God. It's almost as if the Bible knows we can't stand too much of these stories without finding some relief.

But these protective strategies are deeply revealing. Like the horror movies that wanted to talk about the war but couldn't find a way to do so directly, these texts seem to introduce bits and pieces of the horrors of war before swerving back to something more comforting. For the careful reader, however, they leave a mark.

They reveal what we're supposed to be afraid of: war, in these texts, is not the glorious conquest of Joshua, with God overseeing the Israelite army in a bloodless rout of Jericho when the walls came tumbling down. War endures long past the battles themselves, through years of siege, years of exile, and years of trauma.

And after they've reflected on what they're asking us to be afraid of, these texts push us to explore the anxieties that we have underneath. In both of these stories, seemingly regular people—we have no reason to be suspicious of the character of either the unnamed woman in 2 Kings or the psalmist—are pushed to either carry out or wish for monstrous actions upon children. How much would we have to be pushed for this kind of monstrosity to be unleashed in us?

In both instances, the Bible offers an answer to this unspoken question: Precisely when we are pushed into the most monstrous portions of ourselves is when we need to turn to God for deliverance. In the narrative of 2 Kings 6, and the poetry of the psalms, God is the one who can deliver us from both the monsters without and the monsters within, borne of the trauma that these outer monsters inflict upon the world.

Section 4

Horror of the Divine

9 Apocalypse Soon

Most of the stories you hear are about things that happened, maybe yesterday or maybe long ago. But this isn't a story like that—this is a story about what will happen someday. We don't know when, but this is what God has promised lies in store for us.

I know you have things to complain about in your life. We all do. Maybe you don't have as much rich food as you might like on some days and have to get by on vegetables and grains. Maybe you look at others in the city who have more than you do, and well up with envy. Maybe you sometimes think about how unfair it is that, even with all the talent and dedication and faith you have, others seem to get all the good things in life, and you get left behind. Maybe these things are even true.

Even so, you have a roof over your head and walls that surround you every night, and most nights they keep you safe from wild animals and thieves. You have a family that cares for you and a community that helps you remember your history and stands with you when times are tougher. You have what you need.

But it will not always be this way.

We have heard of a time to come when the world will be torn asunder, these walls that protect us will fall, and our only shelter will be underneath the cold night sky. The land will twist around us, breaking and contorting itself into jagged shapes as we watch. The land will beg for water, but will become parched with thirst, and the crops that have fed us will no longer grow.

The land will twist around us, yes, but so will its people. When you take away the comforts that people have become used to, they grow misshapen, the evil that hides in their hearts rises to the surface and they feel justified in letting it run free. After all, in a world where there is nothing to hope for, nothing to look forward to, the choices we make and the ways we treat each other do not matter. There is only surviving to the next day.

And that becomes our lives, surviving and praying that we will open our eyes again to the next day's sunlight. There is nothing more to hope for, nothing more to expect from life, for everything else is gone. We move, because staying still leads to death. We eat what we can find and do not know when we will eat again, because the land has stopped caring for us. We do not know where God is in these days, or when God will come back to care for us again. We are alone in a desolate, forsaken landscape, struggling in a world that is broken and battered under the weight of its transgressions.

I remember my first encounter with this kind of world-shattering apocalyptic imagery. I don't think I was too odd of a child, but I was sure fascinated by death in movies. I remember being in first grade and trying to keep a running body count for the films I cherished most, movies like *Clash of the Titans* and *Jason and the Argonauts.* Morbid, sure, but also just an example of how exciting violence can be. (I'm sure Walter Wink and his theological reflections on the myth of redemptive violence would have something to say about this.)

I was also a burgeoning comic-book fan. My parents had a cottage in northern Michigan, and I always complained about how long the Friday afternoon drive was. So, we'd taken to breaking the trip up by stopping at a grocery store in a small town about a half hour away, and I'd head straight for the magazine shelf in the back of the store. Because on the bottom shelf there were always a few comic books, and I could usually talk my parents into buying one for me.

One afternoon, I gravitated toward a science fiction comic I'd never heard of called *Dreadstar.* It featured a gallivanting space outlaw who was trying to put an end to a war between two intergalactic empires, neither of which was on the side of good. I don't remember any of the details of the issue I picked up, but I have a clear memory of these cosmic villains dropping a nuclear bomb on a huge metropolis, wiping out everyone in it. Dreadstar climbs his way out of the rubble he was buried under and can only whisper, "By the stars! No . . ." when he sees the devastation. The superhero didn't save the day in this issue, and I couldn't count the numbers. I read it over and over again until the cover fell off, enthralled by this right turn into something that didn't seem at home in the superhero genre. While this story doesn't have all of the marks of the apocalyptic genre that we'll talk about in this chapter, the imagery sure would have been at home in something like the book of Revelation.

As you've probably guessed, the bleak campfire story at the beginning of this chapter isn't the prelude to a volume of *The Walking Dead*, or even a more highbrow dystopian apocalyptic novel like Octavia Butler's *Parable of the Sower* or Cormac McCarthy's *The Road.* But it certainly seems familiar from those worlds. It's a somewhat loose retelling of Isaiah 24, from a series of chapters that is often referred to as the "Isaian Apocalypse." Just consider these lines, from Isaiah 24:19–20:

> The earth is utterly broken,
> the earth is torn asunder,
> the earth is violently shaken.
> The earth staggers like a drunkard,
> it sways like a hut;
> its transgression lies heavy upon it,
> and it falls, and will not rise again.

The poetry is devastating; it's not simply a vision of destruction being inflicted upon people, but upon the earth itself. The image of the earth crushed under the sins of its inhabitants is deeply chilling, and—given the climate crisis that threatens to consume the world in the next few generations—more relevant today than the biblical authors could have possibly known.

It's a specific kind of horror, one that's often called apocalyptic. We've come to use this term to mean "the end of the world," or at least "the end of civilization," but that's not quite right. It actually means "an unveiling" or "a revelation." The book of Revelation is *apokalupsis*, where we get our modern word *apocalypse* from. The end of the world is frequently present in apocalyptic visions. But what's more important than that is what these visions show us about the current state of our world—what they reveal. The intent of apocalyptic literature is less to present a vision of the future than it is to peel back the layers that cover the truth about the world we live in today, giving us insight into how the heavens move and God directs all. Apocalyptic visions are meant to provide us with painful, unvarnished truths about the current state of our lives, our society, and our world—and to give us hope that it doesn't always have to be this way.

The apocalypse is a relative latecomer on the biblical genre scene. We talked earlier about the development of the Hebrew Bible, with texts as old as 2000 BCE, but the majority of it was written around the period of the Babylonian exile, in the sixth century BCE. The first apocalypses we have are much later than that; the book of Daniel seems to have reached its final form in the middle of the second century BCE. (For those keeping score at home, the predictions that Daniel 8 makes match up really closely with some of the events of the years between 167 and 164 BCE, but it gets unreliable after that.) For some scholars, it grew out of the prophetic tradition; for others, it's an outgrowth of a particular type of wisdom. Its origins are a bit mysterious, but its function is pretty clear.

The prophets, like Isaiah and Jeremiah, usually envision a time when this existing world will be made right. Injustices will be fixed, the righteous will be lifted up, the wicked will get what's coming to them. God will have a hand in this, of course, but the basic vision is one where this current world gets put in the right order.

But what if things get so bad that we can no longer imagine them being fixed? In that case, the only thing to hope for is that the slate gets wiped clean and something entirely new emerges out of the wreckage. This is the vision that apocalypses hold up for us.

In the Old Testament, we see a sociopolitical situation that gradually grows worse and worse for the people of Israel. The hope of their new temple devolves into a series of more and more oppressive rulers, as a seemingly never-ending stream of empires takes over. (These are the different parts of the statue that Daniel talks about in Daniel 2, and the four beasts that he sees emerging from the sea in Daniel 7.) It became harder and harder to imagine the existing world being made right; so the authors of Daniel, and other apocalypses like the books of Enoch and Revelation, imagine an entirely new world, remade as God would have it be.

Earlier scholars on apocalypse thought it had to emerge from groups that were experiencing severe oppression; more recent sociological studies, taking contemporary apocalyptic movements into account as well, have modified this to say that groups who create apocalyptic texts and adhere to apocalyptic worldviews must be experiencing at least *relative* deprivation. In other words, they might actually come from privileged classes; in modern-day America, many of the groups who have identified with apocalyptic strands of religion are actually quite well off. But they experience themselves as living under oppression, or as being persecuted, even if to an outsider they might look like they're doing just fine.

Interestingly, about the same time as the genre of apocalypse is being formed in the second century BCE, the Jewish religion also starts to develop an idea of life after death—and, particularly, a judgment that comes about in the afterlife. It seems to come from the same impulse. If we don't have justice in this world, there must be justice in the world to come. As it becomes harder and harder to imagine this world meting out justice, we begin to imagine this justice taking place in another world.

We see this same impulse in Isaiah 24, where the entire earth is crushed under the weight of its sins. But if we endure these images of horror, we're left with an image of hope. It begins with the promise that God will bring down both the rulers of earth and the angels in heaven—nothing of the existing power structures will remain. And the natural world is not exempt either, as the passage ends with this series of images:

> 24:23 Then the moon will be abashed,
> and the sun ashamed;
> for the LORD of hosts will reign
> on Mount Zion and in Jerusalem,
> and before his elders he will manifest his glory.

To circle back around to the questions that have guided us throughout this book: What are these passages asking us to be afraid of? The answer here seems fairly straightforward: On the surface, we're afraid of this unveiling, of the earth's being rent asunder and our lives torn apart. But the real message is a little different. Apocalyptic texts tell us we should be afraid of the present, because it's a pretty terrible place to be.

This is the same way that more contemporary pop-culture apocalypses work as well. Starting with George Romero's *Night of the Living Dead*, zombie apocalypses show us a vision of the world falling apart and people trying to build up a new society out of the wreckage—but behind this picture is a sharp critique of how we're living our lives today. In *Night*, a small group of people take shelter from the zombie hordes in an abandoned farmhouse but quickly realize that their fellow human is as heartless—and maybe as brainless—as the ghouls outside. (Fun trivia fact: Romero never calls the monsters zombies in this movie—he used the term *ghouls*.)

At the film's beginning, we're introduced to Barbra and Johnny, siblings who are visiting their father's grave. We see some playful banter between them, learn a little about their relationship and their backstory—all the marks of establishing major characters in the film. But just a few minutes into the movie, Johnny is bitten and turned into a ghoul himself, and Barbra takes shelter in a nearby farmhouse. By the time she gets there, she's almost catatonic—she doesn't have much to contribute to the survivors she finds already holed up in the house. Instead, the mantle of main character is taken up by Ben, a young African American man who seems comfortable taking charge. There's a collection of other characters in the farmhouse; young couple Tom and Judy, as well as a family led by patriarch Harry (whose daughter is ominously not feeling well). Tom and Judy become ghoul food when they make a break to gas up the truck, and Harry spends most of his time trying to boss everyone around and yell ineffectually at people. By the end of the night, Ben is the only survivor—but he meets his end at the hands of a ragtag militia that mistakes Ben for one of the ghouls. The film ends with a chilling sequence of black-and-white photos of this mob disposing of corpses, with Ben's body unceremoniously mixed in with the ghouls.

Overall, the film paints a bleak picture. The ghouls are certainly awful, and they've managed to break apart the comfortable world. But as the people in the farmhouse—especially the men—descend into macho displays of yelling and punching, it's hard not to wonder what's really been lost with the disintegration of society. Is this really what we are at our core? Even more than making us afraid of an impending zombie apocalypse, *Night of the Living Dead* asks us to be afraid of what we are, and of our inability to get along with one another without resorting to violence.

We could go through Romero's entire zombie oeuvre—along with dozens of other more recent imitators—and play this same game. Zombie films, more often than not, give us a vision of a future where society has fallen apart in order to make us afraid of the society we're living in today.

There's a profound truth that apocalyptic movies try to point out, time and time again—we're afraid of chaos, of the lack of order, of our security systems' collapse. We're afraid of uncertainty and not being in control. But when we step back and look at the bigger picture, sometimes the control that we think we have—and the systems that help us feel this sense of control—aren't as great as we think they are. Sometimes we should be less afraid that chaos will knock down our walls and more afraid of how these walls are confining and controlling us. A movie like *Night of the*

Living Dead presents us with a deeply unsettling challenge: *Perhaps we should be a little less afraid of the chaos that might be coming, and a little more afraid of the controlled order that's already here.*

At first, it seems like the Bible's stance toward chaos and order is much more straightforward. God's always on the side of order; chaos is the monster to be struggled against. But when we start pulling at the loose ends of that narrative, the threads start to unravel pretty quickly.

The conflict between order and chaos is first presented in the very opening of Genesis 1, where God fashions the world out of the *tohu vabohu*, the "formless and void" of the pre-creation world. As much as it's a story of creation, it's also a story of ordering—the word divide is repeated throughout Genesis 1. God is taking up all of the formless stuff and putting it into its right place so that we have order, so that we have land and water, sea and sky. But over against all of this is the *tehom*, the deep that darkness covers at the very beginning. In this *tehom*, one might find echoes of *Tiamat*, the chaos monster of other ancient Near Eastern myths who stands against the ordering of the world. Theologian Catherine Keller has argued that we're instinctively afraid of this *tehom*, so much so that we often don't see the possibilities inherent in the pre-ordered chaos. She coined the wonderful neologism *tehomophobia* to describe this fear.

Sometimes, the Bible itself exhibits this *tehomophobia.* But Genesis 1 itself seems to delight in order without necessarily being afraid of chaos; there's no fear in this passage, just wonder at all of the possibilities of the world. And the apocalyptic narratives embrace the chaos as a means of getting through to the other side, to a world where the seemingly ordered world we live in—which is really a world of disorder, even if it has its comforts—is no more. Instead, the chaos that arises out of these sometimes terrifying apocalyptic narratives is a way of helping us move toward something new. Without the disruption, we'd continue to exist in our day-to-day world, frustrated at its injustices but tolerating them because we don't know of anything else. It's only by imagining the chaos that we can begin to see a new way forward.

After Daniel has seen the horrifying visions of the monsters rampaging across the earth, learned of the empires that will fall, and been given the understanding that our wars on earth are mirror images of wars in heaven, he learns that all will be put right in the end. The guide Daniel has had through these visions reassures him:

> There shall be a time of anguish, such as has never occurred since nations first came into existence. But at that time your people shall be delivered, everyone who is found written in the book. Many of those who sleep in the dust of the earth shall awake, some to everlasting life, and some to shame and everlasting contempt. Those who are wise shall shine like the brightness of the sky, and those who lead many to righteousness, like the stars forever and ever. (12:1–3)

It's often thought of as the first unambiguous reference to the resurrection of the dead in the Bible and offers the comfort that there will be something good on the other side of this nightmare. We may be suffering from persecution now, but there will come a time when we'll be rewarded with glory.

Often when we hear about the book of Revelation and the end times, it's a frightening vision of things that are to come, and the biblical story gets transformed into a ham-handed attempt to scare people straight. (Sometimes figuratively, sometimes literally.) We hear this when televangelists offer predictions about when the end is coming, what we need to be doing to get ready for it, and how angry Jesus is going to be when he gets here. But I think this way of talking about the book of Revelation gets a couple of things completely wrong.

First of all, I don't think apocalyptic texts like Revelation are asking us to be afraid of the future—they're asking us to be afraid of the present. What's scary isn't the destruction that will happen in the future, but what these texts and stories show us about what is happening today. Daniel's vision of four beasts rising out of the sea isn't meant to tell us that this will happen someday, but that the empires we are living under today are like these four ravenous, destructive monsters—and it's these empires we should be running from in fear.

And a second point they frequently get wrong is how often they emphasize this recreation as the ultimate triumph of their group. There are a few texts in most apocalyptic visions that sort out winners from losers—and if it were up to me, those would have been left on the cutting room floor. What's most important is the vision of a new creation, a new world being made out of the irredeemable wreckage of the current one. That newness is what we should hold onto.

While Jars of Clay is one of my favorite contemporary Christian bands, I've always cringed at the lyrics to their song "Goodbye, Goodnight," in which they imagine a triumphant procession of the faithful at the end of times. The singer almost sneers at the rest of humanity as he envisions himself and other believers going on up to heaven: "fake a smile as we all say goodbye." If your primary joy is imagining the suffering of others, I think you've missed the most important part of what these texts are trying to say. I don't think they're about the triumph of one particular group, at least not mostly. For me, they're much more powerfully read as being about the triumph of all of humanity and God over the forces of evil.

Many scholars have tried to divide horror movies into those that are fundamentally conservative and those that are progressive. Robin Wood does this when he compares the joyously anarchic films of the 1960s and 1970s to the sodden, restrictive slasher films of the 1980s—the civil rights movement versus the Reagan revolution. And W. Scott Poole does something similar when he discusses movies that support empire versus those that question it—basically, films like *Jaws* that tell us that humanity can overcome and conquer anything, versus those like *The Thing* that question this premise. I think a similar dichotomy is present in how horror movies—and biblical texts of horror—understand our relationship to the cosmos.

In apocalyptic narratives, there are going to be terrifying disruptions, threats of gigantic proportions, and enormous loss in the face of monsters, zombies, and whatever else the universe might throw at us. But what's understood as corrupt is human society. These apocalyptic upheavals are the universe's—and God's—way of putting things back into balance, of rebuilding what had gone off course. It's a vision of a universe that's fundamentally good, even if human society doesn't always (or ever!) manage to stick to this goodness with any kind of consistency.

Sometimes, this optimism can seem buried under the particularities. *Night of the Living Dead*, for example, gets so deep into the rot of contemporary American families and societal racism that it's hard to imagine any positive vision for the universe. The long-running TV series *The Walking Dead* is similar; with every episode, the characters seem to get beat further and further down by zombie persistence and human cruelty. In these cases, it seems like the apocalyptic imagination of our screens and televisions isn't quite as wide as that of the Bible—an imagination that can see past the cataclysms, beyond the wars and the bloodshed, and into the new world that will follow.

It's this act of imagination that is truly the act of hope. If you were to ask the author of Daniel or Revelation what the new world to come would look like—how it would be organized, how resources would be divided, what kind of economic system we'd have—I don't imagine they'd be able to tell you. But if the biblical texts we have are any guides, they would affirm that whatever it is, it's going to be what God intended for this world, and for humanity—something far different than the mess we've created for ourselves. That's something worth hoping for.

10 Ark Encounters at the Edge of the Universe

Sometimes, the most terrifying events are those that are the most unexpected, those events that happen in the midst of joy and celebration and remind us that the universe does not care about our delight. In the midst of happiness, we can be reminded that death can come for us at any time, and that we are seldom more than one small step away from destruction.

This story happened not too long ago, when David had first become king over all of Israel. He was leading a celebration into Jerusalem with the Ark of God, preparing to bring it into his palace as a royal tribute to the grace and generosity that God had shown him and his people. There was all manner of dancing, and singing, and revelry in this procession—by some accounts, our king made rather a fool of himself with how unashamed he was, dancing for God as if no one else was watching.

But this all turned to horror in the blink of an eye. The oxen that were pulling the Ark stumbled, and it began to totter; Uzzah reached out his hand to steady it so that it would not come crashing to the ground. For his devotion to this relic of God, Uzzah was struck dead immediately.

As he fell to the ground, the parade stopped, the lyre players let their instruments fall mutely to their side, cymbals dropped with a final clash onto the dust. Everyone could only stare in shock at this man who had been alive a moment ago, now dead because he had dared touch the Ark.

It mattered not that he had touched it in an attempt to be helpful, that he had tried to steady it out of devotion. All who saw his lifeless corpse, his skin suddenly withered like parched leather and his eyes bulging like overripe grapes, knew that God accepted no rationalizations for this act—he had touched the Ark, he had breached the chasm between the human and the divine, and because of this his life was forfeit.

The people had seldom seen their king so angry. He shouted to the heavens, demanding to know why this impious act was so unforgivable as to require a good man's death. He received no answer.

Powerless before the divine, David could think of nothing to do but refuse to bring the Ark into his palace.

My first experience of cosmic horror was long before I had any idea of what cosmic horror was. Really, before I even knew what horror was. I didn't know quite what I was watching or why I was so mesmerized, but looking back on it, I recognize the same kind of stirrings that I feel when I read some of H. P. Lovecraft's best work, or John Langan's brilliant novel *The Fisherman*, or the book of Job. It tapped into deep fears about the nature of the universe in a way that my six-year-old brain couldn't process but knew was amazing.

This was a year or so before the VCR really hit the marketplace; I had one friend who had one, but he lived in the rich neighborhood on the other side of town, so I didn't get to go over much. My family was lucky enough to have HBO, but if you missed a movie in the multiplex in those days, there weren't many options aside from waiting until it came around to one of the pay channels. Every month, I scanned the program guide as soon as it arrived in the mail to keep track of what I needed to see in the coming month.

But it was also the time of second-run movie theaters, these strange and always somehow disreputable places that would show movies that had left the theater, usually for a dollar and with fifty-cent bags of popcorn. The closest one to us was—I kid you not—in the back of a Showbiz Pizza Place. Showbiz was a Chuck E. Cheese knock-off, sort of like if *Five Nights at Freddy's* hadn't yet become self-aware of how creepy it was. In the back of this pizza place was a small room with about twenty-five or thirty folding chairs set up, a projector, and a small screen. When I reflect back on things like this from my childhood, I'm reminded that the

1980s are definitely a foreign country. I have often wondered what my life would be like today if I could take advantage of one-dollar tickets (and fifty-cent popcorns) at places like this. I'm sure I would be a very different person.

This night, I was playing with blocks in my room and heard my parents having what sounded like a very serious conversation. My bedroom door was open, so I could see my parents down the hall talking in hushed tones, with some back and forths and some side-to-side headshaking on the part of both my parents that seemed to indicate they were weighing something very important. As they broke the huddle, my dad clued me in on what the conversation was about.

"There's a movie in the theater that we think you'll really like. It's about a guy who runs around the world looking for treasure, being chased by a bunch of bad guys." It was called *Raiders of the Lost Ark*, and this brief description was enough to have me hooked. I don't remember exactly how else my parents described it; in hindsight, I know they were concerned about how violent it was, but also thought it was pretty freakin' cool and knew that I'd love it—so maybe a little excessive violence was worth it. This is a trade-off I have often thought of when considering what movies to share with my kids.

There's a little religious mysticism in the beginning, but I think I paid about as much attention to it as most kids pay to the exposition of any movie. (Yeah, quit talking so you can start running around and punching things!) After the boring talking, most of the movie is a straight-up adventure yarn, with fight scenes in the Cairo marketplace, lots of machine guns that don't seem to hit anything except Nazi cannon fodder, and highly improbable vehicle-to-vehicle acrobatics. I was loving every minute of it. But it was the film's conclusion that really threw me for a loop.

You probably remember the plot, so I'll try to move through it as quickly as possible. Indiana Jones has been tasked with locating the Ark of the Covenant before the Nazis do. The Nazis believe it's some kind of weapon of mass destruction, and the US government isn't sure but doesn't want to take any chances. Indy succeeds, but the Nazis manage to intercept it. After some twists and turns, Indy and his partner-in-archaeology Marian find themselves captives, being marched through a remote island to a location where the Nazis can open the Ark and see what kind of a weapon they've got. And boy, do they ever find out.

Indy and Marian are smart enough to close their eyes after the Ark is opened—Indy remembered the Old Testament passages about not being able to look upon the face of God and live. (Probably the most famous iteration of this idea is Exodus 33:20, where Moses asks to see God's face on top of Mt. Sinai but is rebuffed. Instead, God offers to run by so that Moses can catch a glimpse of his backside. Really, I swear—that's what it says! Modern translations often gloss over this as God's "back," but I think that's more polite than the actual Hebrew.) But the Nazis, as is their wont in popcorn movies, are not so smart. At first disappointed that there's only dust in the Ark—the tablets of the Ten Commandments three thousand years later—they become enthralled when ghostly spirits begin to emerge. These spirts swirl around the Nazis, at first playfully, but—in a change signified by the score's shifting to a minor key and one of the ghost's face's transforming from that of a young woman to a hideous skeleton—turn violent and slaughter the whole Nazi battalion. Some are electrified, some explode, others have rays of light that shine through their bodies and out their eye sockets. It's horrifying and seems to come from a completely different genre than the rest of the film. I mean, one of the Nazis' faces literally melts off like candle wax, his runny-egg eyes sliding down his cheeks.

As a six-year-old who'd experienced my share of good guy versus bad guy fights, I didn't have a basket to put this in. I remember feeling a little terrified, but mostly exhilarated and fascinated. That was the scene that my mind kept replaying over and over after the lights came up and we left the creepy pizza parlor to head back home. It might have been just that the level of gore was higher than what I'd seen before; I can't think of any other PG movies that culminate in a full-on face-melting scene. That might have been a part of it, but I don't think that's the whole story of my fascination with that scene. I think it has more to do with the ideas it taps into about the universe.

It's really a scene of cosmic horror, tacked onto a story that is mostly just an action-adventure yarn. Not only is there a shift from action to horror, as evidenced by the gore, the supernatural elements, and even the score (in hindsight, John Williams' score in this scene seems to be channeling a slightly more melodic version of Bernard Herrmann's famous shower-scene score for *Psycho*, with the short, staccato string bursts sounding like aural stabbings), but it's also a shift to a particular type of horror, one that's less concerned with what happens to individual protagonists than it is with what the plot developments reveal about the nature of the universe. Usually in cosmic horror, the big reveal is that the universe is run by forces who might be entirely hostile to humans—or, perhaps even worse, think humans aren't even worthy of consideration.

This corner of the horror genre is usually traced back to H. P. Lovecraft, the early twentieth-century American author whose imagination brought us Cthulhu, the Elder Gods, and a whole host of professorial protagonists who learn more than they wish they had. (While there's much that's brilliant in Lovecraft's writing, I feel I can't talk about him without mentioning that this revelation is often tied to some idea of racial hierarchy or genetic purity; the guy really believed that white men of a certain class pedigree and Anglo-Saxon background should be at the front of the pecking order.) It's not a monster who invades normalcy, such that the monster can be chased away and everyone can go back to their suburban lives. Once the protagonists have lived through the plot of a Lovecraft story, they can't ever look at the night sky again. In the best examples of the genre, the stories have this same effect on their readers.

Movies like *The Thing*, *Annihilation*, *The Mist*, and *The Lighthouse* all tap into this mode, as does the final sequence of *Raiders of the Lost Ark.* In *Raiders*, it seems clear that the Ark is a divine power that's beyond our ideas of good and evil. I never doubted for a second that if Indy and Marian had continued watching after it was opened, they would have been swallowed up by it just like the Nazis were. It's an object that is supposed to be holy, but which proves fatal for anyone who gets too close to it. Rather than the soft, cuddly image of God that we're often given in Sunday school, this presents God as a powerful, uncontrollable force that we need to keep our distance from. Get too close, and our eyes might start running down our faces.

The Hebrew Bible has many places where God is relatable, approachable, and a comforter for people in need. I don't want to give the idea that what we learned in Sunday school is completely wrong! But if we read the Bible all the way through, it's incomplete, because there are also plenty of places where God relates to the people more like that final scene of *Raiders of the Lost Ark.*

A couple of these scenes even involve the Ark. I'm guessing that somewhere in the writing team of George Lucas, Philip

Kaufman, and Lawrence Kasdan, one or more of these folk knew their Bible pretty well. One of the most terrifying is the story retold at the head of this chapter; David's triumphant procession with the Ark into Jerusalem, which quickly turns to terror when Uzzah touches the Ark in an attempt to steady it. (The story is found in 2 Samuel 6.) He is struck dead instantly. There's no indication that he touched the Ark disrespectfully or had any motive other than making sure this holy relic didn't crash to the ground. But his intentions didn't matter. He touched the Ark, and it was immediately fatal.

David recognizes what this means. Verse 8 summarizes plainly: "David was angry because the Lord had burst forth with an outburst upon Uzzah." For a deity who is supposed to be defined by being "slow to anger" (Exodus 34:6 and Psalm 86:15, among many other places in the Old Testament), God shows a strikingly quick trigger finger. For a deity who is supposed to offer forgiveness to the faithful, God responds to Uzzah with a definitive lack of forgiveness or opportunity to repent. Instead of offering a word of thanks for protecting the Ark, God lashes out in anger.

David's response indicates that he isn't just upset over Uzzah's death or frustrated with disagreement over God's choice. Instead, David seems to understand that this incident means that God is a different kind of God than David thought God was. While the affirmations about God's grace and kindness might be true, David, Uzzah, and the rest of the procession got to see a different side of God. What does this shadow side of the divine mean for how we understand the world and our place in it? For Lovecraft, how he really wanted to chill readers was to make them think about "listening, as if for the beating of black wings or the scratching of outside shapes and entities on the known universe's utmost rim." Do we have any reason to believe that these shapes and entities wish us well?

This is the key question that cosmic horror asks, a question that the Bible doesn't shy away from either. There are more than a few examples of God acting irrationally, violently, or unfairly—at least from our perspective as humans. Did you know that, after commissioning him to free the Israelites from bondage in Egypt, God tried to kill Moses while he was on his way to talk to Pharaoh? It's a brief episode at the end of Exodus 4, and it's dropped in with hardly any context or explanation. And then after God's assassination attempt is rebuffed, everyone keeps going on with the story like nothing happened. It's bizarre and deeply chilling.

Psalm 8 gives us a view of humanity and the world filled with awe and wonder. The Psalmist looks up at the heavens, the "work of [God's] fingers," and marvels that God "has made us a little lower than the angels." There's God, and then just below that there's humanity. In this beautiful partnership, humans serve as the steward of creation. It's the pinnacle of the Bible's anthropology, a psalm that's built around the wonder of feeling humanity has a special place in the universe, a place of honor and privilege.

But when we see how Uzzah's life can get snuffed out for the simple act of touching God's Ark, we're forced to rethink this picture—or at least to acknowledge that it's complex. Here, the hierarchy is more like God, and then everything else. And we're so far below that an individual like Uzzah hardly even matters. If God can decide on a whim to kill his chosen servant Moses, it seems likely that there's a ton about how the universe works that is simply beyond our comprehension.

Let's step back and ask what cosmic horror is asking us to be afraid of. In Lovecraft's most famous tales, the monsters are the Old Ones, or the Elder Gods—beings who have either been asleep or absent for millennia but are starting to rouse from their slumber or find their way back to earth. They're terrifying beings, so terrifying that Lovecraft frequently runs up against the limits of language when trying to describe them. They're more than we can comprehend. So clearly, we're meant to be afraid of them.

But more than that, we're meant to be afraid of what they tell us about the universe and our place in it. Psalm 8 tells us that we're the pinnacle of creation, just a little lower than divine beings. That's how we like to think of ourselves. Instead, Lovecraft posits a world where these other creatures—they might be aliens, they might be gods, but they're so much greater than humanity that the distinction really doesn't matter much—are the rulers of the universe, and we're insignificant enough to barely be worth their notice. We're only alive because we're not worth their attention. Lovecraft's work and other narratives of cosmic horror ask us to rethink the entire structure of the universe and realize that our ideas of it as a benevolent place built to support human thriving are childish fantasies. We're only alive because we don't matter.

This isn't too far away from the message we get from Uzzah's death, or from God's final speech in the book of Job, or God's sending angels to massacre the people of Israel as punishment for David's crime of taking a census. (A census, it should be noted, that God asked him to take! It's in 2 Samuel 24. The author of the book of Chronicles was evidently so disturbed by this that, when he retold the story in 1 Chronicles 21, he changed the instigator of the census from YHWH to Satan!) God is so holy that the only thing we can do to save our lives is to stay away. If we attract divine attention, we risk being smited for a crime as innocent as steadying a falling Ark—or for no crime at all.

It's fascinating to me that the Hebrew Bible can hold both of these views of humanity in tension. We're made in God's image (Genesis 1:26), and we're a little lower than the angels/God (Psalm 8:5). But at the same time, we're not holy enough to approach the divine; if we do, in fact, we risk death. And even when we're not talking about divine spaces, sometimes there are places in the world that just don't care about humanity. In the speech from the whirlwind at the end of Job, God regales Job with stories of the goats that live in mountains far above where humans can live, and the sea monster Leviathan that lives in the depth of the sea, far away from where humanity is welcome. God sums this idea up in a more mundane statement: God brings "rain on a land where no one lives, on the desert, which is empty of human life" (Job 38:26). If the point wasn't clear enough, God brings it home: this is "to satisfy the waste and the desolate land," not for any human purpose. The world is bigger than we are, and we matter less than we think we do.

The Bible presents us with both of these views: we are the pinnacle of creation, and we are utterly meaningless in the cosmic scope of things. I don't think it's helpful to play gotcha, where we put these two kinds of verses side-by-side as evidence that the Bible is fallible. Somehow, both of these things are true at the same time—but in the biblical world they're only true when they're held together, one truth in the right hand and one in the left, creating a synthesis that transcends any simple addition.

This is where the Bible really parts ways from contemporary understandings of cosmic horror. In Lovecraft, there's no Psalm 8 to balance out the terrifying indifference of the Old Ones, no Genesis 1:26 to juxtapose with the Elder Gods. There's just cold, dark space, with beings that are so much greater than us as to be an entirely different form of creation. But in the Bible, humanity is both belittled and exalted, just as God is both violent monster and tender comforter. These truths are too big to be encompassed by any single, straightforward proposition.

It's that sense of overwhelming vastness, both physically and intellectually, that I respond to so strongly in cosmic horror. I think of times in literature and film where the world opens up in a way that's terrifying but also offers an entirely new canopy for our thoughts and emotions. In Stephen King's novella *The Mist*, and in the Frank Darabont movie that was based off it, there's a fantastic scene near the end. The story follows a cataclysmic event that has unleashed an all-encompassing mist on a small New England town, with horrible monsters lurking inside. A group of survivors has spent most of the story holed up in a supermarket, and a small band has finally escaped to see if they can drive far enough to reach the mist's end. At one point, they stop their car when the ground starts shaking, then look in awe out the window as an enormous beast strolls past. It's part wooly mammoth, part Lovecraftian god, but large enough that they can barely see its head. And it pays no mind to them whatsoever, just stomping along its way. I've always found that indifference so much more chilling than if it were angry, or hostile, or if it turned into an action-packed scene where they had to run from it or try to face it with explosives or whatever. They don't even try.

Raiders of the Lost Ark's climactic scene with the slaughter of the Nazis taps into the same emotion for me, the same set of feelings as the end of the book of Job, or that brief scene with Uzzah and the Ark. As soon as the Ark is opened, we've left the world of predictable action narrative behind and gone into a world that's darker, more unstable, and that causes us to think about what the world we live in means. Up until this point in the movie, Indy had been the traditional action hero—he might take a beating, but we know he's going to come out the other side of it alive. But with the opening of the Ark, we have a different truth revealed. His only chance is to look away and hope the divine powers that the Ark unleashed don't notice him. Welcome to the horrors of the universe, Indy.

As a six-year-old, I thought I knew what kind of movie I was watching. Indiana Jones isn't technically a superhero, but he might as well be. Nothing seems to kill him, and he can figure out how to get through any impossible death trap or overwhelming army. But suddenly at the end of *Raiders of the Lost Ark*, he's powerless. There's nothing he can do but shut his eyes and wait for the divine storm to pass him over. In this final scene, it's clear that Indy isn't the superhero my six-year-old self thought he was.

It's a helpful corrective, both for action movies and for our understanding of what it means to be human. Along with telling us that we are made in God's image, Genesis 1:26 tells us that we have been given "dominion over" all the animals on the earth. For centuries, this has been used as a rationale for plunder, a way to excuse our destruction of the natural environment by telling ourselves that the whole world is just here for our use. If we think we're a little lower than the angels, it's not too big of a leap to convince ourselves that everything on this planet is here to serve us.

These glimmers of cosmic horror in our tradition are an enormously important counterweight to this viewpoint, a reminder that we might not be as important as we think we are. While the logical endpoint of Lovecraft's work might be despair, I'd argue that the cosmic horror of the Bible is doing something different. It's giving us the shadow side of Genesis 1:26 and Psalm 8, a dark reflection that serves to temper whatever grandiose ideas we might have about ourselves. Look in some corners of the Bible, and there's nothing in the depths of the cosmos but a terrifying void. But look in other places, and we have an exalted place within a well-ordered universe and are given special responsibilities by God. Take both at the same time. When we're in despair, we can remember the unique calling we've been given. And when we start to think we're the masters of the universe, we might remember Uzzah and his hand on the Ark. Or Indiana Jones with his eyes shut.

Conclusion

Does the Bible Mean to Scare Us?

The idea that the Bible contains horror stories might seem surprising, or even outrageous, at first, but I hope these pages have shown that it's not as controversial an idea as it first seems. But this still leaves us with a lingering question that I've been turning around in my mind for over a decade now. Does the Bible think these are horror stories? In other words, when the original authors, human and divine in whatever combination you believe the Scriptures were written, wrote these pages, were they trying to scare us? And would the people who have heard or read them in their original contexts receive them this way?

There are challenges whenever we take the lens of a contemporary genre and project it backward into history. The genre of horror fiction, as we think of it today, likely started with Mary Shelley's *Frankenstein*, with the Gothic romances of the nineteenth century as its clearest antecedent. And for horror movies, you'd probably look to the 1930s Universal monster movies, if not the cycle of German expressionist films from the 1920s like *Nosferatu* and *The Cabinet of Dr. Caligari.* Those are the first places where you have something that really shares a lot of features in common with how we understand horror literature and movies today, and where we can begin to trace a direct line to these more contemporary works. There's a huge gap between that lineage and the thousands-of-years-old stories of Scripture—they come from a different culture, a different way of writing, and are clearly trying to communicate what they see as theological truths as their primary goal. There's a huge gulf of difference.

But that's still not quite getting at the fundamental nature of the question. Horror stories are about finding ways to try to scare their audiences, using the tools of whatever medium they're working within. Is there enough evidence to say that, in the same way that contemporary novels and movies are trying to scare their audience, so too was the Bible in some places?

I think there is. While I'm not making an argument for any of the authors of the Bible as being an ancient Stephen King, there's enough evidence to plausibly say that scaring its readers is one of the items on the Bible's agenda. Along with instilling a wide range of other emotions, of course, but fear is one of the responses the Bible tries to draw out from us.

I think we can demonstrate this by looking at the number of techniques the Bible uses that have substantial overlap with contemporary modes of horror. There's not only the use of monsters, but also the focus on the grotesque, the rhetoric of intimidation and fear, and plotlines that even emulate the rising suspense leading to a sudden reveal that mirror the plots of horror. These are all techniques that are designed to instill fear in the audience, engineered to raise goose bumps and leave the reader feeling shaken after they've put down the book or stopped listening to the speaker tell the tale.

I think it's a strong case that horror isn't simply a modern category that's being imposed on these ancient texts (though of course we should recognize the cultural and literary differences between what's in the Bible and what we see in the movie theaters). I think that gets us closer to some interesting conclusions, but there's still one major question left to explore:

Why in the world would the Bible want to do this?

If the biblical authors had wanted to—or been so inspired by God—they clearly could have written a book that was nothing but happy puppies and rainbows. (Though there is at least one rainbow in the Bible.) But that's not the book they wrote. So why is this the book we have in front of us? Why are all of these tales of horror found interpolated among the stories of uplift and encouragement?

I can think of a few reasons, none of which seems sufficient by itself, but they seem like parts of a larger story.

First, horror stories are fun to read and to listen to. It's why we tell stories by the fireside, and why every Halloween haunted house tries to give itself a history and a backstory, instead of just a series of startles. These stories are fun. While it might be hard to recognize this when you're deep in the bowels of Leviticus, the Bible really does try to be something that engages, something that makes us want to keep turning the ideas it presents to us over in our minds. That's why it's full of stories and poems, rather than just lists of what we should and shouldn't do. While those lists might have made things easier in some ways—and the Bible does have some passages that are little more than lists of laws and rules—these lists are also easier to ignore and don't keep us coming back to them as readers. I think the reason that we still read the Bible today, and why I have a job as a biblical studies professor, isn't just that it's full of timeless truths. It's also that the stories and poems are genuinely engaging and keep us returning to them over and over again to see what else we might be able to glean from them. Stories do that for us, so it makes sense that the Bible would have stories of all different types to continually keep us engaged, surprised, and wanting to read more. I think part of it is the simple acknowledgment that horror stories are fun, particularly when they're juxtaposed with other types of stories that arouse different emotions.

But there's also got to be something more profound to it than that. "Fun" certainly isn't the only goal of the Bible, or even the primary one.

Another piece of this puzzle is that the Bible intends to surprise us and encourage us to see the world in different ways, and that's a goal at which horror is particularly adept. The whole point of religion is to reorient our value system in life, to convince us that how we think we've understood the meaning and purpose of everything around us isn't sufficient. (Or might be altogether wrong.) Think back to our discussion about the monster as being what disrupts normalcy, what threatens the routines and patterns of everyday life. That's what Christ explicitly said he came to the world to do—"I have not come to bring peace, but a sword" (Matthew 10:34)—and it's also the basic pattern of a horror narrative. Everyday reality is disrupted so we can examine what that reality actually means, and if it's worth fighting for, or if we might be better off figuring out a different way to do things.

Even more than trying to surprise us, the Bible tries to help us understand that the world as we see it is not all there is. Whether that's a divine reality that's just outside our senses, or life after death, or simply the fact that our rational minds can't understand everything that makes the world work, part of the Bible's goal is to help us broaden the way we see the world and the universe, even if we can't fully grasp what we're being shown with our limited human brains. Horror excels at helping us take those imaginative leaps into the unknown, at pushing us to experience things beyond what we can fit into a rational equation. Horror helps us to imagine.

Decades ago, biblical scholar Walter Brueggemann coined the phrase "the prophetic imagination." He imagines a push and pull of the biblical text between the royal consciousness, which wants to keep everything safe and static, and the prophetic imagination, which is always pushing us into new possibilities, helping us to imagine a world that's better than the one we currently inhabit. Many scholars and pastors—myself included—have found this an extraordinarily powerful framework; as I was considering whether to start a graduate degree in seminary, it was one of the books that gave me the final nudge into my Master of Divinity program. It's been an incredibly generative set of ideas, leading to all kinds of explorations of how the biblical text both attempts to effect and resist change at various points.

Over the years, I've come to believe that part of the prophetic imagination—part of how the Bible calls for change and helps us imagine new realities—is through horror. Throughout this book, I've tried to make the case for horror as a key component of this imaginative strand of the Bible. When we want to shine a light on how our society as it currently exists is failing so many of us, we imagine it falling apart, being overrun by zombies or torn apart by the great red dragon. When we struggle with the violence of our society and try to seek refuge in an imagined past, folk horror traditions remind us that the past has always been a violent place, and that a retreat to the good old days of yore won't solve anything (because those days really weren't so good).

In many ways, it feels like the Bible's use of horror breaks down into a few distinct categories:

1. Sometimes, the Bible uses horror as a simple cautionary tale. Don't do this, or this terrible thing

will happen to you. It's a well-worn use of horror, from fairy tales to slasher movies. Sometimes, the laws in Deuteronomy read like this.

2. At other times, the Bible uses horror as a means of pointing us toward the horrors of the world we've built. Apocalyptic literature works like this, and so do the horrific war passages from Kings.
3. And yet a third inflection is when horror is used to help us think about the universe in a different way. The monstrous portrayals of God are like this; so is the end of the book of Job, and other places where we're asked to re-envision our place in the cosmos.

In all these cases, horror tries to teach us something and to help us think about things in new ways. It might be that we could get there through another means than horror, but horror proves to be an effective pedagogical tool—when we know how to read it right.

So, what does this mean for us as readers of the Bible? I hope you'll come away from this book with a few takeaways. First, don't be afraid of the horror in the Bible—except in the appropriate ways that you're supposed to be afraid of horror. Maybe more precisely, don't be afraid to acknowledge that there's horror in the Bible. And consider that this may not be just our response to an ancient text that sometimes seems kind of weird—it might be what the text is actually trying to do. There *is* horror in the Bible.

Next, try to pay attention to what this horror is trying to make you afraid of and what pre-existing anxiety it's trying to help you reflect upon. There's a monster, or a war, or a cataclysm of some kind, but what is this horror's relation to the world as we know it? What facet of our society or human behavior is this putting under threat—and is that a bad thing or a good thing? Are we looking at the kind of horror that wants to reassure us that the world will be okay, or the kind of horror that tries to convince us that the only way forward is radical change, either of societal structures or how we think about things?

For me, a big part of the excitement of horror is that it doesn't lead to straightforward answers to these questions. Even though it's a genre, with conventions and norms just like any other, it can be used in a multitude of ways, for a wide range of purposes. In the end, the horror of the Bible is part of the conversation this book wants to have with us, one of the many tools it uses to help us rethink how we understand our relation to each other and to the divine. So be scared of the Bible, because the Bible is asking you to be scared! And then think about what you're being asked to be scared of, and what that might mean. And then ask what you might do with that new knowledge.

When we look at things this way, being scared of the Bible doesn't mean that we have to reject it or that it's somehow less holy than we thought it was. It's an acknowledgment that it's a richer, deeper book than we might have thought, one that has comfort and grace but also disgust and terror. It's a conundrum that only becomes richer as we acknowledge these contradictions.

The King James Bible that I started to read cover-to-cover when I was ten wasn't the last Bible I got from my grandmother. She gave me another one just before she died; it was the Bible that had belonged to her husband, and the one he would use for weddings and funerals. It's full of his handwritten notes, including a roughly scratched out order of service in the blank pages at the end. I used this order of service after her passing, when my family asked if I would officiate her graveside service. This Bible still had all the stories of violence and war that we talked through in the pages you've just read, all of the monsters and people doing unkind things to each other. But it's also the Bible that has the twenty-third psalm and the passages from First Corinthians that comforted my family as we mourned our loss.

So I hope developing your own hermeneutics of horror will help you get through some of these more troubling passages of the Bible, help you find a way into and back out of the texts that seem to offer no way forward. But I also hope that you can hold onto whatever comfort and encouragement you've found in its pages—because those are just as real as the horrors.

Appendix

The Trauma (and Horror) of the Old Testament

The stories from the Old Testament are old—far older than the book itself. A lot happened to them from their first telling to the time they found the form that's been transmitted to us. You might have heard something like this before, but it's still surprising to dig deep into what, exactly, that means. We don't have all the answers to these questions—many of them are lost to history. Even so, we've got some pretty good guesses, some theories that seem to explain why we have the strange text that we do, and an idea of the historical realities that might have made the text come together in this way. It's a story of the trauma of history—and a story that explains why the Bible, in so many ways, reads like a horror story.

The Old Testament covers the story of the first man and woman—Adam and Eve—all the way to the building of the Second Temple, which happened around 515 BCE. (The books of Ezra and Nehemiah narrate this, and some of the prophetic texts such as Haggai, Zechariah, and Malachi have clear references to this event as well.) It seems likely that the oldest stories and prayers were told orally before they were written down, and it seems clear that there were revisions and additions made even after the stories were put down on paper. (Or papyrus, more accurately.) In short, this isn't a book that came together the way we think of a modern book being written, where a single author sits down at their computer, starts typing with the first word, and ends with the last. It was a process of a committee working on a shared document over a period of several thousand years. You might think of it as a precursor to a document in Google Drive that everyone's editing, except even that understates how complex the process probably was; there were probably ten different Google Docs being worked on at the same time, but some of them got destroyed or people lost the passwords along the way. And then, centuries later, someone decided we should probably just have a single version, so that we're all reading from the same page. The book of Daniel is just one example that we looked at in a previous chapter—a mishmash of two different languages, different genres, and a number of cultural contexts. And chapters that got added into the Greek version but not in the Hebrew. Just about every book in the Old Testament is at least this complicated.

That goes a long way toward explaining why so much of it feels disjointed and strange. The book may be the Word of God, but it's also the product of a committee. If you've ever served on a church board, you know that even the work of God can get really messy when it's subjected to Robert's Rules of Order. And when at least two people on the committee are acting like this church board meeting is their only obligation in life for the next month, they're pretty happy to keep it going as long as possible.

But it's when we get into the history behind the text that we can really start to see how the Old Testament is, in many ways, a story of horror.

In earlier scholarship, the idea was that the "Bible" as we know it started to get compiled and finalized during King Solomon's rule, sometime in the tenth century BCE. (Biblical scholars like to use centuries—for most people, that would be around 900 BCE.) Then, later stories got added on for the next few hundred years. Not many biblical scholars buy that theory anymore. While most would agree that there are remnants of earlier stories, poems, prayers, and other traditions, it was a few hundred years afterward that the priests and scribes really started to fix their traditions into a final form and put together what we think of as the Old Testament today, probably closer to 500 BCE.

And it was all in response to an unthinkable, horrifying event in history—one that threw the entire nation of Israel into chaos and threatened its very existence. More than that, it threatened everything they thought they knew about God.

Israel was never a very big country and found itself in the middle of a bunch of warring nations. At first, this was

Egypt. Then it was Assyria. Later, the armies of Babylon (now located in modern-day Iraq) rose up to become the dominant power in the region. And still later, the armies of Greece and Rome fought for supremacy in the region. Each of these nations, put into symbolic motion as the form of the monsters in the book of Daniel, did their best to lay claim to Israel as part of their territory; most of them more or less succeeded. But the most traumatic of these occupations was that of Babylon.

Babylon's method was to invade, destroy what they could and plunder the rest, then drive most of the people into exile. This way, there wouldn't be anyone left to resist. Only the poorest people remained after Babylon invaded, with new rulers installed by Babylon. This happened to Israel in 598 BCE, when Babylon laid siege to Jerusalem; after a decade of soft warfare, they finally destroyed the city and the temple in 587. Some of the scattered people rebuilt communities in Babylon, others fled to Alexandria. They'd stay there until the whole region was conquered by the Persian empire in 539; according to the biblical books of Ezra and Nehemiah, King Cyrus of Persia allowed the Jewish people to return to Jerusalem and build a new temple. (Scholars debate how accurate this account is—these books might have been an attempt on the part of upper-class Jewish writers to curry favor with the new boss.) So the people returned to Jerusalem and rebuilt the temple. Some of the writings of the Old Testament are clearly post-exilic and talk about the building of the new temple. But many of them seem likely to have been written, or at least put into their final form, during the period of exile. For many scholars, this event hangs over the entire Old Testament.

It's hard to imagine how terrible this event would have been. Losing your land, your home, and your community is awful enough. But for the Israelites, the temple wasn't just the place where they worshipped—it was where God lived. The inner sanctum of the temple was referred to as the "Holy of Holies," and it was where God dwelled on Earth. So having this temple destroyed raised all kinds of questions. If the Israelites' God was truly the God of all the earth, how could this happen? Why didn't God protect his dwelling place—and protect his people? Was the god of Babylon actually more powerful than the god of Israel, so that Israel's god had actually been defeated?

In many ways, I think the entire Old Testament is designed to explore these questions. (To wrestle with them, if you will.) It's a series of reflections on what faith means, the power of God, and how God's power manifests in the world—and how this power doesn't always show itself in the ways we might expect. Over and over again, the Old Testament tells stories of God making a way out of no way, pulling hope out of the most hopeless situation.

The clearest summation of the typical "plot" of horror that I've ever heard comes from film scholar Robin Wood. He writes that all horror stories are about how "normalcy is threatened by the monster." The rest of the story is about trying to defeat that monster so that normalcy can be restored. The Old Testament begins with what the writers considered "normal"—the Garden of Eden, where humans are in direct relationship with their creator, where there is no conflict or strife, and where the needs of all living creatures are met. This is what is, or at least should be, normal.

This normalcy gets disrupted, first by the serpent, then by the violence of Cain against his brother. And we see it being disrupted again and again. When we read it from this perspective, the Old Testament is all about a longing to return to that normalcy of the Garden—and about how we live in the meantime when we're far from home. Even the boring laws that tell us when we have to put down an ox for being too violent (basically, if he's a repeated gorer) are about how we live together when where we're living is not the ideal world we wish we were living in. They're about how we make the reality we find ourselves in as close to normal as we can.

And this brings us back to the exile and the invasion by Babylon.

This experience of being far from home—far from what should be normal, in the parlance of Robin Wood and horror theory—is a through-line that starts in Genesis and goes all the way to the end of the Old Testament. The story of Adam and Eve is about losing home and being cast out into an unfriendly world. The story of Abraham is about trying to find a new home, someplace that can substitute for the garden paradise that was lost. The story of Moses, particularly the wandering through the wilderness, is a clear parallel to the experience of exile the Israelites were living through.

Often, horror narratives emerge as a way to try to address some national trauma, some societal anxiety that's too big to fit within the small spaces of our own lives. Whether it's the trauma of the Great Depression that fueled the Universal monster movies of the 1930s, the anxiety over nuclear war that laid the groundwork for the science fiction horror movies of the 1950s, or America's role in the Vietnam War that served as the impetus for the dark and hopeless horror movies of the 1970s, horror has always played a major role in navigating these moments of cultural crisis—right up until the current boom in horror, which seems driven by the fear and chaos that Donald Trump has injected into America.

If the work of modern scholarship is correct, and these documents were primarily formed during the exile, then the Old Testament is a perfect example of how a community can respond to trauma through storytelling and through tales that can (at least at times) veer toward the horrific. Sometimes, we need to have our fears dramatized, either through a storyteller or in the printed word on the page, or on the big screen at the multiplex, to start to think about how we might handle them. When we take these fears and tilt them just enough to turn them into a story, we've got a chance to face them.

Narrative Bibliography

Hey there, reader! This essay is a behind-the-scenes look at some of the writings that have helped guide me along this strange path. If you're interested in learning more, read on—but if you've had enough already, you have my permission to put the book down and consider yourself as having finished reading *Scared by the Bible.*

I was working at an indie bookstore in Northern California as a twenty-two-year-old grad student when I stumbled upon a book called *Men, Women, and Chain-Saws: Gender in the Modern Horror Film* by Carol J. Clover (Princeton University Press, 1992). It was the first time it had occurred to me that people could take horror seriously and has cast a large shadow over all of my academic pursuits since. A similar seismic shock hit me when I was studying apocalyptic literature in my PhD program and reading a book by Anathea Portier-Young called *Apocalypse Against Empire: Theologies of Resistance in Early Judaism* (Eerdmans, 2011). There's a brief footnote in the book that references monster theory and mentions a couple of books in the fields of Bible and religion that explore this idea. One book was Timothy K. Beal's *Religion and Its Monsters* (Routledge, 2002; second edition 2022), and in many ways everything I've written has been an attempt to chase after this book.

What follows are my attempts to show my work for this book, to give some insights into the books that have helped to shape my thinking on these ideas. If you're interested in pursuing any of these topics further, you could do worse than starting with some of these titles.

Introduction

I maintained my involvement with the church throughout my twenties, though often felt adrift and wondered if I was just continuing to attend out of habit. My pastor at the time, Rev. James Truesdell, recommended I read Marcus Borg's *Meeting Jesus Again for the First Time* (HarperCollins, 1994); I don't think it's an overstatement to say that this was the book that kickstarted my journey into seminary. Borg argues that we have a tough time transitioning from the childish God of Sunday school to a mature, adult understanding of God. In many ways, it's an updated version of a book my mother loved: J. B. Phillips's *Your God Is Too Small* (Simon & Schuster, 1953), which argues that we too often think of God as something like a divine Santa Claus or policeman.

Peter Enns' *The Bible Tells Me So: Why Defending Scripture Has Made Us Unable to Read It* (HarperOne, 2013), is a cogent and very readable argument about how we fundamentally misunderstand the Bible as a book of instructions, when that's not at all what it was intended to be. The Steve Wiggins' quotes are from his essay "The Theological Origins of Horror," in a book I co-edited (with John W. Morehead) called *Theology and Horror: Explorations of the Dark Religious Imagination* (Lexington Books/Fortress Academic, 2021), quotations from 25–26.

For questions of genre, Andrew Judd has written an outstanding introduction: *Modern Genre Theory: An Introduction for Biblical Scholars* (Zondervan, 2024). Lots has been written on Mikhail Bakhtin, and his book *Problems of Dostoevsky's Poetics* (University of Minnesota Press, 1984; translated by Carol Emerson) is the best place to start with reading his own writings. Gary Saul Morson and Carol Emerson's *Mikhail Bakhtin: Creation of a Prosaics* (Stanford University Press, 1990) is an excellent introduction to Bakhtin's work, with emphasis on his theories of genre.

I've written about the *Tales from the Crypt* comics and HBO series as reflections of Deuteronomistic systems of reward–punishment in *Lurking Under the Surface* (Broadleaf Books, 2022); there's also a great essay by Kevin J. Wetmore, Jr., called "Justice through the Resurrection of the Dead: Moral Theology and Eschatology in EC Comics" in a volume I co-edited (also with John W. Morehead) called *Horror*

Comics and Religion: Essays on Framing the Monstrous and the Divine (McFarland, 2025).

The question of how horror is related to affect has taken center stage in the last decade or so. Adam Charles Hart, *Monstrous Forms: Moving Image Horror Across Media* (Oxford University Press, 2020), has been particularly influential in my thinking. He argues that horror is not primarily a narrative genre, that what defines it more than plot points or structure is its direct appeal to the emotions. Xavier Aldana Reyes' *Horror Film and Affect: Towards a Corporeal Model of Viewership* (Routledge, 2016), is an important work in this trajectory.

Chapter One

My favorite overview of early horror cinema and how it developed into the Universal horror films of the 1930s is Kendall R. Phillips' *A Place of Darkness: The Rhetoric of Horror in Early American Cinema* (University of Texas Press, 2018).* For a history of horror that's more centered on the studio system and the personalities that drove these movies, David Skal's *The Monster Show: A Cultural History of Horror* (Farrar, Straus, and Giroux; revised edition 2001) is still tough to top. An interesting historical note—many of the silent films mentioned in this chapter are short because

* The 1910 version of Frankenstein was produced by Edison Studios, directed by J. Searle Dawley.

early silent films were confined to a single reel of film, which could only hold about twenty minutes. It wasn't until a little later in the development of silent films that movies began to stretch out over multiple reels.

The reference to Tzvetan Todorov is to the Russian scholar's work *The Fantastic: A Structural Approach to a Literary Genre* (Cornell University Press; 1975, translated by Richard Howard).

The question of where horror comes from has been speculatively explored by Paul A. Trout, *Deadly Powers: Animal Predators and the Mythic Imagination* (Prometheus, 2011). Matthias Clasen, *Why Horror Seduces* (Oxford University Press, 2017), uses contemporary psychological research to reach the conclusion that the primary attraction of horror is its role in training our response systems to perform at a higher level in the case of encountering a real-world threat. Brian Keene, in his Patreon post "That Rough Beast Returns" (February 24, 2024), writes that "when the world is full of very real horrors, there is a strange comfort to be found in make believe horrors" (https://www.patreon.com/posts/that-rough-beast-99115797). For him, it's more about psychic survival—reassuring ourselves that there might be a way out of the mess that our world is becoming/has become.

Darryl Jones, *Sleeping with the Lights On: The Unsettling Story of Horror* (Oxford University Press, 2018) is a highly readable history of horror, pushing far back beyond the usual origin point of Gothic fiction. Similarly, Edmund P.

Cueva, *Horror in Classical Literature: "On a Profound and Elementary Principle"* (University of Wales Press, 2024), finds the roots of horror in classical Greek and Roman literature. The Steve Wiggins quotation is from the same chapter cited in the notes for chapter 1.

A fun popular-level introduction to American horror films is Jeremy Dauber's *American Scary: A History of Horror, from Salem to Stephen King and Beyond* (Algonquin Books, 2024). Robin R. Means Coleman, *Horror Noire: A History of Black American Horror from the 1890s to the Present* (Routledge, 2011; second edition 2023) is a much-needed corrective to traditional texts that either view race as of secondary importance to the horror genre or overlook it completely.

Victoria Nelson's book *The Secret Life of Puppets* (Harvard University Press, 2001) is a fascinating book, though it relies heavily on a firm distinction between high- and popular culture that I don't think can be sustained. Jason Ray Carney has put Nelson's work (along with that of Thomas Ligotti) into conversation with my own in an essay for the *Los Angeles Review of Books*, "Does Horror Infect or Protect?: On Brandon R. Grafius's *Lurking Under the Surface*." Douglas E. Cowan has made this point numerous times throughout his writings and interviews, but this quotation is from *America's Dark Theologian: The Religious Imagination of Stephen King* (New York University Press, 2018), p. 6. A broader overview of Cowan's thinking, and perhaps a better place to start reading his work, is *Sacred*

Terror: Religion and Horror on the Silver Screen (Baylor University Press, 2008), one of my earliest influences and generally regarded as the first book on horror films and religion published by a university press.

Biblical scholars often regard Jacob as a trickster, most notably Susan Nidditch's classic work *Underdogs and Tricksters: A Prelude to Biblical Folklore* (HarperCollins, 1987). A more recent work, focused exclusively on Jacob and much more technical in nature, is John E. Anderson, *Jacob and the Divine Trickster: A Theology of Deception and Yhwh's Fidelity to the Ancestral Promise in the Jacob Cycle* (Eisenbrauns, 2011). The standard overview of biblical narrative and its style is still Robert Alter, *The Art of Biblical Narrative* (Basic Books, 1981; revised and expanded in 2011). Meir Sternberg's book on biblical narrative, which features a lengthy discussion of gaps in biblical stories such as that of David and Uriah, is *The Poetics of Biblical Narrative: Ideological Literature and the Drama of Reading* (Indiana University Press, 1985).

In 32:24–25 (32:25–26 in the Hebrew; the verses in this passage are one off in the English version), Jacob is described as meeting a "man," an איש ('ish). In vv. 28 and 30 (Hebrew 29 and 31), the term used first by the being himself and then by Jacob is *elohim*, אלהים, which can mean either God or one of God's divine beings (as in Psalm 8:5, Hebrew 8:6). For me, the ambiguity about who, exactly, Jacob was wrestling with serves to deepen the uncanny nature of this passage. I refer to the English verse numbering, here and throughout the book.

The phrase "disorienting dilemma" is associated with the work of Jack Mezirow; see, for example, his *Learning and Transformation: Critical Perspectives on a Theory in Progress* (Jossey-Bass, 2000). I am grateful to my doctor of ministry student Trent Elders, whose work on disorienting experiences with clinical pastoral education students by way of wilderness encounters first introduced me to Mezirow's ideas.

Chapter Two

Jeffrey Jerome Cohen's essay is almost thirty years old, but whenever a paper is presented on monsters at an academic conference it's a good bet that it's going to be based on these seven theses. The essay was originally published as an introduction to the volume he edited called *Monster Theory: Reading Culture* (University of Minnesota Press, 1997), which is where the term *monster theory* originated. It's also anthologized in Jeffrey Andrew Weinstock's excellent edited volume *The Monster Theory Reader* (University of Minnesota Press, 2023), which has all of the foundational texts of monster theory gathered between two covers. Noël Carroll's *Philosophy of Horror: Or, Paradoxes of the Heart* (Routledge, 1990) is the other main source of theorizing about monsters.

While there's been some great work on Daniel and all of the monsters in this wild and wonderful book, there isn't much that explicitly draws on monster theory. Anathea Portier-Young's *Apocalypse Against Empire* is a very theory-informed look at the monsters in the text, and Paul A. Porter's *Metaphors and Monsters: A Literary-Critical Study of Daniel 7 and 8* (CWK Gleerup, 1983) helped me to think about how we might look at these monsters as metaphorical assemblages rampaging through the text. The C. L. Seow quote is from the excellent scholar's commentary on Daniel in the Westminster Bible Companion series (Westminster John Knox, 2003), p. 103.

Both Timothy Beal in *Religion and Its Monsters* (cited above) and Stephen T. Asma, *On Monsters: An Unnatural History of Our Worst Fears* (Oxford, 2009) talk about the Latin root of *monster* as pointing us toward the idea that monsters are messages.

The Robin Wood quotation is from his oft-anthologized essay "An Introduction to the American Horror Film," first published in 1979, at a time when few scholars or critics were taking horror movies seriously. It's been enormously influential on horror theory in general, and my thinking in particular. It's collected in *Robin Wood on the Horror Film: Collected Essays and Reviews* (Wayne State University Press, 2018), among many other places.

The chapter features a reference to the "uncanny valley," which might be a phrase that's vaguely familiar to readers—or maybe not. The uncanny valley is the influential idea introduced by Masahiro Mori, an important thinker in the space of robotics, ethics, and religion. If something—a robot or puppet, for example—is obviously non-human, we can respond to it as an object. If it is extremely human-like, we might have an "affinity" for it, in Mori's words, recognizing what it shares with us. But between these two extremes is what Mori refers to as the uncanny valley, where an object falls that is simultaneously too human and not human enough. While widely available, a good source for the article is in Jeffrey Andrew Weinstock's edited volume *The Monster Theory Reader* (University of Minnesota Press, 2020), pp. 89–94.

There's been a lot of interesting work on H. P. Lovecraft and philosophy, and even some on Lovecraft and theology. Graham Harmon's *Weird Realism: Lovecraft and Philosophy* (Zero Books, 2012) offers detailed readings of passages from Lovecraft's stories to explore how the author attempted to imagine the unthinkable and explore ideas that were outside the bounds of language. The volume edited by Austin M. Freeman, *Theology and H. P. Lovecraft* (Lexington Books/ Fortress Academic, 2022), is full of fascinating essays.

Mark S. Smith's book *The Priestly Vision of Genesis 1* (Fortress Press, 2010) is a great discussion of the struggle between chaos and order in Genesis's creation story; another classic text is Jon Levenson's *Creation and the Persistence of Evil: The Jewish Drama of Divine Omnipotence* (Princeton University Press, 1988).

Throughout the ancient Near East, it was common for kings to associate themselves with gods of order and their opponents with chaos monsters. Gregory Mobley, *The Return of the Chaos Monsters—and Other Backstories of the Bible* (Eerdmans, 2012), gives a very readable introduction to this.

If you're feeling brave and want to dive deeper, C. L. Crouch's *War and Ethics in the Ancient Near East: Military Violence in Light of Cosmology and History* (de Gruyter, 2009) is a detailed scholarly treatment.

Chapter Three

The distinction between anxiety and fear goes at least as far back as Danish philosopher Søren Kierkegaard, laid out in his 1844 book *The Concept of Anxiety* (Princeton University Press, 1980; translated by Reidar Thomte and Albert B. Anderson). I think Kierkegaard would find it rather surprising to find his theory being applied to surface- and deep-level analyses of horror films.

There's an entire cottage industry of academic books on the subject of how to interpret the Bible. My favorites are the ones that don't prescribe what to do or what theological truths you should reach, but that talk about the skills and practices we can develop to become better readers. In my work as a seminary professor, I've taught William Brown's *A Handbook to Old Testament Exegesis* (Westminster John Knox, 2017). Side note: *Exegesis* literally means "pulling out of" the text; sometimes, scholars will distinguish the practice of interpreting (exegesis) from the theory of interpreting (hermeneutics), but I see them as words that describe different parts of the same process. I wouldn't attempt to teach hermeneutics without also teaching exegesis, and vice versa.

(I'm assuming that if you're reading the bibliographic notes in the back of the book that you're looking to seriously geek out. Doing my best to help with that.)

The approach I take with hermeneutics is to look at the different "lenses" through which we can read a text, lenses that arise from our own social location, experiences, and personalities. So I introduce students to feminist interpretations, postcolonial interpretations, African American interpretations, materialist interpretations, and a number of others. For me, horror is just another one of these lenses that we can use.

A couple of fun notes that didn't quite fit in the body of this chapter: Though director John Carpenter famously used his home location of Southern California as a stand-in for the film's midwestern suburb, the eagle-eyed viewer will be able to spot a couple of palm trees.

Film scholar Carol J. Clover noted that most slashers end with a single girl being left to face the killer alone; she dubbed this character "The Final Girl," a moniker that has lived on in popular culture in places such as Grady Hendrix's tongue-in-cheek novel *The Final Girl Support Group*, about a group of Final Girls who find themselves being targeted by a new killer. See Clover's *Men, Women, and Chain-Saws: Gender in the Modern Horror Film* (Princeton University Press, 1992). I wrote about slashers and the Bible at great length in my academic book *Reading Phinehas, Watching Slashers:*

Horror Theory and Numbers 25 (Lexington Books/Fortress Academic). It was my dissertation, so be warned that it's not as fun to read as its title might suggest. But hey, if you're reading these bibliographic notes, you might be the book's target audience. After you see the book's price tag, you won't hurt my feelings if you get it from the library.

I should also note that this chapter dances around the edges of "authorial intent," which is a sticky topic. John Carpenter isn't a fan of the interpretation of *Halloween* I've laid out here. This problem becomes even more acute when we're talking about biblical texts, and Paul isn't around to offer clarifying remarks on the passages he wrote. I still think it's valid to offer interpretations that authors may or may not have considered on the grounds that this is the magic of creativity—when we write something, it's more than the sum of ourselves as an author. That's at least doubly true if you believe the Holy Spirit was involved in the writing of the biblical texts.

The best defense of the artistic merit of the *Friday the 13th* movies I've read is horror scholar Wickham Clayton's *See! Hear! Cut! Kill!: Experiencing Friday the 13th* (University of Mississippi Press, 2020). He argues for a much more sophisticated worldview based on the films' use of POV, editing, and other cinematic techniques. In some ways, even Clayton's book makes my point—if you want to admire slasher films, you have to look somewhere other than narrative.

Chapter Four

Kevin J. Wetmore, Jr., discusses *The Conjuring*'s R rating in his Devil's Advocates volume on *The Conjuring* (Liverpool University Press), p. 15. He notes that the Motion Picture Association of America gives the film's rating reasons as "sequences of disturbing violence and terror." He summarizes: "[I]t gets its power from what it does not show."

A really fun history of film censorship and the developing standards of taste is Sheri Chinen Biesen's *Film Censorship: Regulating America's Screens* (Wallflower Press, 2018). My editor, Carl Bromley, has some great stories to tell about how the video nasties circulated on bootleg VHS tapes in the 1980s United Kingdom. He was apparently his school's underground distributor. If you want to dive deeper into the history of *The Texas Chainsaw Massacre*, including more anecdotes like the one I shared about its re-rating, check out Stefan Jaworzyn, *The Texas Chain Saw Massacre Companion* (Titan Books, 2004). Jaworzyn reports that Hooper, demonstrating a rather amusing lack of awareness of what he had created, had originally hoped the film would be given a PG rating because it didn't have much overt on-screen violence.

Xavier Aldana Reyes, *Contemporary Body Horror* (Cambridge University Press, 2024), is a succinct introduction to the genre. David Scott Diffrient's *Body Genre: Anatomy of the Horror Film* (University of Mississippi Press, 2023) explores all the ways that bodies are involved in the viewing and production of horror movies. David Huckvale's *Terrors of the Flesh: The Philosophy of Body Horror in Film* (McFarland Publishing, 2020) is another great exploration of body horror.

If you're feeling brave and looking to dive deeper into Leviticus, the work that towers over everything else is Jacob Milgrom's three-volume opus for the Anchor Bible Commentary series, running well over 2,500 pages in total. A much less daunting way to start is with James W. Watts, *Ritual and Rhetoric in Leviticus: From Sacrifice to Scripture* (Cambridge University Press, 2007).

Chapter Five

I was at a conference at Texas State University a number of years ago called "Gods and Monsters" which tried to bring together scholars interested in religion, monsters, and horror from various disciplines. A Hebrew Bible scholar (working on his dissertation at the time) named Leland Merritt presented a paper on Genesis 34 and rape-revenge films; it's been revised into a chapter of an edited volume that emerged from that conference, called *Religion, Culture, and the Monstrous: Of Gods and Monsters* (Lexington Books, 2019), edited by the conference's co-conveners Natasha L. Mikles and Joseph P. Laycock. For a deeper dive into how Wes Craven's oeuvre can be interpreted through a theological lens, including the director's early days at an evangelical college, his never-published novel (!), and even his attempt at a theological porn film (!!), check out *Theology and Wes Craven*, edited by David K. Goodin (Lexington Books/Fortress Academic, 2023), part of the same "Pop Culture, Theology, and Religion" series that includes my co-edited *Theology and Horror.*

Dennis Olson's commentary on the book of Judges is in volume 2 of *The New Interpreter's Bible;* the quote is from page 726 in the twelve-volume edition (Abingdon Press, 1998). This series is highly readable but also written by scholars who know their stuff; as a seminary student, it was the first commentary I tried to read all the way through. (I didn't get through all twelve volumes, but I read a lot of it.) It's a good place to go if you're looking for some succinct thoughts on a passage but want a little more than a straightforward devotion.

Joy A. Schroeder's book *Dinah's Lament: The Biblical Legacy of Sexual Violence in Biblical Interpretation* (Fortress, 2007) looks at the frequency, throughout the centuries, with which scholars have tried to interpret these biblical passages of sexual violence in ways that blame the woman. Rhiannon Graybill's *Texts After Terror: Rape, Sexual Violence, and the Hebrew Bible* (Oxford University Press, 2021) is an outstanding work of scholarship that reads these texts through contemporary affect theories, arguing that many of the stories of the Bible are intentionally "messy and icky," and that we should pay attention to those emotions.

A profoundly moving exploration of the tension between forgiveness and justice is Miroslav Volf's *Free of Charge: Giving and Forgiving in a World Stripped of Grace* (Zondervan, 2006). Volf argues that without the anger that we see God expressing in the biblical text, there can be no hope for justice in this world, but that focusing on justice rather than vengeance is a constant struggle.

Chapter Six

The starting point for thinking about folk horror is Adam Scovell's book *Folk Horror: Hours Dreadful and Things Strange* (Auteur Publishing, 2017). Scovell tries to take this disparate genre and find some common ground, and he manages to use landscape and conflicts between the traditional and modern to tie together films such as *The Wicker Man*, *Blood on Satan's Claw*, and *Witchfinder General.* Another great overview, with a focus that shifts from horror to the gothic, is Dawn Keetley's *Folk Gothic* (Cambridge, 2023). There have been a number of books and articles on *The Wicker Man*, but a very helpful and readable introduction is Steve Wiggins' volume in the Devil's Advocates series (Liverpool University Press, 2023), which reads the film as both folk horror and holiday horror, for its close associations with May Day. The same series also includes a volume on *Witchfinder General* by Ian Cooper, and one on *Blood on Satan's Claw* by David Evans-Powell. I love the Devil's

Advocates series, and not just because I wrote the volume on *The Witch* for it.

Depending on which version of the Bible you're reading—Jewish or Christian—you could find the book of Judges in different places. In Christian versions, the book of Ruth usually followed Judges, since Ruth begins by introducing its setting as "In the time when the Judges judged." In the earlier Hebrew version, Ruth is found near the end of the Bible, along with Ecclesiastes, the Song of Songs, and the other books of the "Megillah," each of which is tied to a particular festival in the Jewish tradition. In the Hebrew, Judges is right in between Joshua and Samuel, part of what is referred to as the "Former Prophets."

Recently, Andrew Judd has read Judges 19, the genuinely awful story of the Levite and his concubine, as a horror story, with the mob gathered around the house as a zombie horde; see *Modern Genre Theory: An Introduction for Biblical Studies* (Zondervan, 2024), 107–116.

Chapter Seven

There's lots of scholarly work on demons in the Bible; a highly readable place to start is Esther Hamori's chapter on "Demons in God's Ranks" in her book *God's Monsters: Vengeful Spirits, Deadly Angels, Hybrid Creatures, and Divine Hitmen of the Bible* (Broadleaf Books, 2023). You could also lose plenty of hours paging through *The Dictionary of Deities and Demons in the Bible* (Brill, 1995; second edition 1999).

Steve Wiggins, *Nightmares with the Bible: The Good Book and Cinematic Demons* (Lexington Books/Fortress Academic 2021), is a fascinating scholarly look at how biblical demons have made their way into popular culture. If you've got access to a university library, there's a great article on demons in contemporary culture by Gregory Stevenson in my co-edited volume (with John W. Morehead) *The Oxford Handbook of Biblical Monsters* (Oxford, 2025).

Zachary Doiron's work was what really drew my attention to the evangelical roots of *The Conjuring* in a pair of articles that are both available online: "Possession, Politics, and Patriotism: The Influence of Christian Nationalism and Evangelical Horror Tropes on *The Conjuring* and *The Conjuring 2*" in *The Journal of Religion and Popular Culture*, vol. 35 (2023), no. 3; and his critical review of *The Conjuring 3: The Devil Made Me Do It* in *The Journal of Gods and Monsters*, vol. 3 (2022), no. 1.

If you're interested in scholarly analysis of exorcism rituals, Joseph Laycock is the author to read. His co-written book (with Eric Harrelson) *The Exorcism Effect: Horror, Religion, and Demonic Belief* is outstanding and has some discussion of both the real-life Ed and Lorraine Warren (demon hunters of *The Conjuring* films) and the backstory of the case that *The Conjuring* was based on. Laycock also edited *The Penguin*

Book of Exorcisms (New York: Penguin Books, 2020), which collects primary source texts on exorcisms.

Chapter Eight

In the last decade or so, moral injury theory has developed to describe the injury faced by returning soldiers who have been ordered to commit acts (or witnessed acts committed by others) that they know are wrong. It's distinct from trauma, since it's not something inflicted on you—it's a betrayal of your deep sense of your moral self by people in authority. In biblical studies, Brad Kelle has applied this theory to many of the war texts in the Hebrew Bible, looking at Saul as suffering due to the immoral commandments given to him by God, as well as looking at how some of the psalms and other texts attempt to provide rituals for healing from moral injury. It's well worth reading. Brad E. Kelle, *The Bible and Moral Injury* (Abingdon, 2020).

Not to get too deep into the weeds—although, again, maybe that's what you're looking for if you're reading these notes—but there's quite a debate among biblical scholars about how much of what we know of David's reign can even be considered historical. For a fairly large contingent, most of it is an exaggerated take on historical occurrences; for many scholars, David was much closer to a tribal chieftain than the king of a developed nation. See, for example, Steven

L. McKenzie, *King David: A Biography* (Oxford University Press, 2000).

W. Scott Poole's outstanding book *Wasteland: The Great War and the Origins of Modern Horror* (Counterpoint Press, 2018) is a great read; you'll learn a ton about silent and early talkie horror films and how they connect with cultural movements of their time.

Walter Brueggemann has been an extremely influential biblical scholar and theologian. His work on the psalms is particularly noteworthy. A good summary of this work is his book *From Whom No Secrets Are Hid: Introducing the Psalms* (Westminster John Knox, 2014); the quotation in this chapter is from page 98.

Chapter Nine

Walter Wink, *The Powers That Be: Theology for a New Millennium* (Doubleday, 1998), talks about how deeply embedded it is in our psyche that we can fix things with violence, and that violence can sometimes be righteous when in defense of a good cause. Once you realize how damaging this mindset is, it's difficult to watch Hollywood movies in the same way. Leave it to us scholars to make everything less fun.

The essay that got me thinking about the connection between zombies and hope is Kelly J. Murphy's chapter "The End Is (Still) Around: The Zombie and Contemporary Apocalyptic

Thought," the last chapter in the volume she co-edited with Justin Jeffcoat Schedtler, *Apocalypses in Context: Apocalyptic Currents through History* (Fortress, 2016). It's a great history of the zombie, but also connects the apocalypticism of zombie movies to apocalyptic movements throughout history.

The standard scholarly introduction to apocalyptic literature—readable for students and non-specialists, if you've got some patience and aren't planning on taking it to the beach—is John J. Collins' *The Apocalyptic Imagination: An Introduction to Jewish Apocalyptic Literature* (Eerdmans, 1984; the third edition in 2016 is greatly expanded and recommended). Scholars still don't know exactly how apocalyptic literature came to be. Paul D. Hanson, *Dawn of the Apocalyptic: The Historical and Sociological Roots of Jewish Apocalyptic Eschatology*, revised edition (Fortress Press, 1979), sees the apocalyptic tradition as emerging from the prophetic tradition; Gerhard von Rad, *Wisdom in Israel* (SCM Press, 1972; trans. J. D. Martin), suggests it emerged out of wisdom circles. These works of literature were clearly something very different from what came before.

"Relative Deprivation" is a phrase from Stephen L. Cook, *Prophecy & Apocalypticism: The Postexilic Social Setting* (Fortress Press, 1995). George W. E. Nickelsburg, *Resurrection, Immortality, and Eternal Life in Intertestamental Judaism and Early Christianity*, expanded edition (Harvard University Press, 2007), is a thorough overview of the development of ideas concerning life after death and the texts that show the gradual development of these ideas.

When I'm checking on things like whether "tehom" and "Tiamat" are really cognates, my go-to first source is *The Dictionary of Deities and Demons in the Bible*, referenced in the notes to chapter 7. David Tsumura, *Creation and Destruction: A Reappraisal of the* Chaoskampf *Theory in the Old Testament* (Eisenbrauns, 2005), thinks we create far too many connections, and that water in the Hebrew Bible is just water, but I don't think that's very much fun (as well as deriving from an overly literalistic way of reading the text). Catherine Keller's *The Face of the Deep: A Theology of Becoming* (Routledge, 2003) is a wonderfully playful exploration of how uncomfortable chaos makes us, even as readers, and how we seek to push it out in favor of order.

W. Scott Poole in *Dark Carnivals: Modern Horror and the Origins of the American Empire* (Counterpoint Press, 2022) argues that horror movies are either supportive of or resistant to empire. Movies that are triumphant, that suggest evil can be overcome by hard work and government institutions, are insidiously supportive of empire in all its forms.

Chapter Ten

The chapter title is a reference to the evangelical amusement park that is structured as a recreation of Noah's Ark, presenting a literal reading of the creation as happening in seven (twenty-four-hour) days. James S. Beilo, *Ark Encounter: The Making of a Creationist Theme Park* (New York University Press, 2018), takes an anthropological approach to explore what this theme park can teach us about fundamentalist culture and worldviews.

In addition to Lovecraft's short stories—"The Call of Cthulhu" is the place to start, and probably the only one you need to read unless you're really into it—Lovecraft also wrote a work of nonfiction called *Supernatural Horror in Literature* that tries to lay out his theories of what distinguishes cosmic horror from its predecessors. The essay, originally published in 1927, is in the public domain; hence, you can buy a discount-priced paperback from Wildside Books (2011) or go deluxe and get the annotated version edited by preeminent Lovecraft expert S. T. Joshi (Hippocampus Press, revised and updated in 2013). The quote is from page 28 in this annotated edition. I'm also a big fan of Eugene Thacker's "Horror of Philosophy" trilogy, *In the Dust of This Planet*, *Starry Speculative Corpse*, and *Tentacles Longer Than Night*, all published by Zero Books. He argues that horror helps us come to terms with ideas that we can't process rationally.

I discuss the truly weird passage of Exodus 4 in more depth in my book *Reading the Bible with Horror* (Lexington Books/Fortress Academic, 2020), pp. 129–31, and recommend it for readers who think this book doesn't have enough footnotes. Psalm 8 has some really interesting translation questions. What the New Revised Standard Version translates as "God" in the King James Version is "the angels"—either one could be accurate. The Hebrew is *elohim*, which literally refers to "divine beings," sometimes God, sometimes the gods of other nations, sometimes the spirits that are the helpers of God that evolve into angels later on in the religious tradition.

Lynn White Jr. was the first scholar to argue that the Bible is responsible for our giving ourselves permission to destroy the environment, in his influential article "The Historic Roots of Our Ecological Crisis," *Science* 155 (March 10, 1967): 1203–07. The article spawned an entire movement of ecological criticism, associated perhaps most closely with the late Norman Habel and his "Earth Bible" commentary series.

Conclusion

The Prophetic Imagination was originally published in 1978 but has been updated many times since. The most recent edition is the 40th anniversary edition (Fortress Press, 2018). It was another of the books that really pushed me into seminary.

A lot of this conclusion is me trying to think through some thoughts that will be developed more fully in my forthcoming academic book *Concerning Dust and Ashes: Affects of Horror in the Hebrew Bible*, scheduled to be published by Oxford University Press in 2026. You get an advance preview in this chapter.

Appendix: The Trauma (and Horror) of the Old Testament

David M. Carr, *Holy Resilience: The Bible's Traumatic Origins* (Yale University Press, 2014) was highly influential in developing my thinking on the relationship between the biblical writings and the trauma of history. Another fascinating work is David Janzen, *Trauma and the Failure of History: Kings, Lamentations, and the Destruction of Jerusalem* (Society of Biblical Literature, 2019). Janzen focuses on how the books of Kings and Lamentations depict (or don't) the destruction of Jerusalem, and argues that the historical narrative of the book of Kings can't process this trauma, so it has to ignore it; in contrast, the fragmented poetic discourse of Lamentations is able to begin the process of raging and grieving.

Congratulations for making it through to the end of these notes! Gold stars and extra credit all around. Seriously, the person who reads through the bibliographic notes at the end of a book is the kind of person I'd like to have a drink with sometime. Thanks for sticking through it to the end.

Acknowledgments

When I first decided to smuggle my love of horror into my PhD program in biblical studies a dozen years ago, it was a leap of faith—there were only a few scholars doing work like this. I hold Timothy Beal and Amy Kalmanofsky in gratitude as the scholars who paved the way, and am continually thankful to Timothy Sandoval, my dissertation advisor, who's not a fan of horror movies but trusted me enough to support this leap.

In the years since then, I've been privileged to have so many conversations among those similarly drawn to the monstrous and the horrific in the Bible and religion more broadly: John Morehead, Kelly Murphy, Natasha Mikles, Leland Merritt, Jessi Knippel, Seth Pierce, Matthew Brake, Eric Jarrard, Matthew Rindge, Rhiannon Graybill, Esther Hamori, Steve Wiggins, and many more. Studying Bible and horror has gone from a lonely place to one of the most engaging corners of the scholarly world. I'll always be grateful to Richard Walsh, Scott Poole, and Douglas Cowan, who were among the first established scholars to take interest in my work, and helped give me the encouragement to keep plowing forward.

My agent, Philip Turner, has shepherded a number of my books into the world, and has helped tremendously in helping me think through how I translate my scholarly work into something that a broader audience can engage with. At Morehouse Publishing, Carl Bromley has been the best editor I could have hoped for—I'll eat barbecue and talk horror with him any day. While Phil Marino has moved on from Morehouse, I remain grateful to him for having seen something in my rather scattered book proposal, and pushing me to clarify what I really wanted to say. The rest of the team at Morehouse has been tremendous to work with, including Anita Manbodh in Marketing and Mark Powers on the production side.

And, of course—thanks to all who've picked up this book and gone on this journey with me! I hope it's been a small comfort in these monstrous times we're living in.

—brg